UMBERTO FORTIS

JEWS AND SYNAGOGUES

VENICE
FLORENCE
ROME
LEGHORN

A PRACTICAL
GUIDE

75 COLOUR PLATES

Library of Congress Catalog Card. Number 72-93070
© Copyright 1973 - N.E. 1984-2004 by STORTI EDIZIONI - VENEZIA
Printed in E.U. - All rights reserved

The itinerary we suggest aims at making better known certain aspects of the history of the largest and most important Jewish Italian communities, by visiting old and new synagogues and museums of art. It can easily be combined with a visit to the various cities, since it truly takes up little time, yet offers a glance at a different world and adds something extra to the ordinary tourist round. Thus, for Jews of today, the encounter with the Ghetto will have the savour of an ideal return to the past, while, for non-Jews, it will be a fascinating novelty.

S. S. N. 67
S. S. N. 67bis

A 11   A 12   km 105

FLORENCE

km 252

VIA AURELIA
S. S. N. 1
km 317

LEGHORN

Cover: Ostia Antica. Synagogue: Architrave with Jewish symbols

VENICE: The Ghetto, the 5 major synagogues, among the oldest still existing (p. 31 fwg.). Museum of Jewish Art (p. 69)

FLORENCE: The Great Temple (p. 77) in Moorish style. The Jewish Museum

LEGHORN: The very modern Great Temple (p. 93 fwg.)

ROME: The Great Temple (p. 101 fwg.) in Assyrian-Babylonian style.
The permanent Exhibition of the Community (p. 118) and at

OSTIA: The oldest known synagogue in the world today (p. 123 fwg.)

A 4 A 13 A 1

km 214

VENICE

ROME

VIA DEL MARE km 28

VIA CRISTOFORO COLOMBO km 31

OSTIA ANTICA

Venice. Museum of Jewish Art: TheThiq - Case for the Scrolls of the Torah

THE JEWS AND ITALY

Among the lands in which the Jews settled during their dispersion, ever since the centuries at the beginning of the vulgar era, Italy was certainly one of the countries where they led a relatively tranquil and serene life. Even though there was no lack of somewhat unhappy periods of hatred and violence, nevertheless the terrible persecutions that rained upon Jews in many other European countries never occurred in Italy. There were many anti-Jewish regulations, many defamatory accusations, segregations, but often certain regulations existed only in theory and were not put into practice. Thus, environmental conditions, the not violently hostile relations with the Italian population, in the course of centuries favoured the cultural, artistic and economic development of some Jewish communities, who in turn contributed to the development of the nation of adoption. Moreover, something happened in the single communities which did not occur elsewhere; although coming from different parts of the world, with differing uses, rites and customs, the Jews succeeded in amalgamating and blending together in unity, avoiding the danger of internal strife and at times establishing connections even between different cities.

Although the first relations between Jews and Italy go back at least to the epoch of the *Maccabees* (2nd cent. B. C.) when the ambassadors of Judas Maccabaeus reached Rome, following which many Judaeans came to Italy for political and commercial reasons, it was nevertheless in the age of Pompey, after the conquest of Jerusalem, that the first Jewish community unit was constituted in Rome (1st cent. B. C.): slaves and freed prisoners, these soon became small craftsmen and tradesmen, joined in time by co-religionists brought by *Titus* after the destruction of the Temple (70 A. D.). During the early days of the **Empire**, their conditions, even in the communities of southern Italy which were soon added to Rome (Bari, Otranto, Venosa), as in the Roman *"Sinagogai"* (small communities), were fairly favourable, excepting difficult moments under *Tiberius and Claudius*. Often confused with the early Christians, the 30,000 or so Jews resident between Trastevere, the Suburra and Porta Capena soon made their spiritual influence felt, just as there were quite a few conversions to Hebraism of Romans attracted by Jewish customs, the sabbatical repose, the use of circumcision, the internal union, so there was no lack of acts of violence towards them, dictated by contempt of cults so strange to pagan eyes. The Jews had, however, autonomous communities, with their own leaders, their own cemeteries in the catacombs, the remains of which still exist. Famous ones are those of *Vigna Randanini, Monteverde, Via Appia* on whose tombstones, now in Roman museums, apart from names, one sees the commonest Jewish symbols. But then, apart from Rome, the communities of *Ravenna, Milan* and those of southern Italy and inland were also important. The first difficulties came with the acceptance of **Christianity**, which provoked restrictions on Jewish liberty and violence on the part of the people against places of worship, and secondly when

Costumes of German Jews of the Middle Ages

Costume of Paduan Merchant of German origin

Costume of Levantine Jew in Venice

Costume of Venetian Pedlar of the Eighteenth Century

the Empire was divided in two which meant that anti-Jewish regulations existing in the East were also applied in Italy. But the subsequent **barbarian invasions**, while bringing fear and hardship, did not cause perturbation, rather, during that of the Goths (5th cent.) the emperor *Honorius* helped the Jews, respecting their shabàth and cults and repealing many restrictions; and *Theodoric*, king of the Ostrogoths, like his successors, while urging Jews to be converted, always opposed acts of violence against them. It was, however, a brief period, for when *Justinian* fought the Gothic war (535), the reign of Byzantium extended again over a great part of Italy; the anti-Jewish legislation of the East and the conditions of the Jews worsened. Such limitations however oppressed them but little; the *Longobards*, in fact, fresh invaders in 568, once converted to Christianity, were not hostile to them nor did they insist on forced conversions. From then, one might say the life of the Jews was conditioned by the policy of the papacy, which assumed an ever-growing importance. Pope **Gregory the Great** was kind, though averse to the Jewish religion: he was always opposed to violence and forced baptism, persuading them to keep alive the rights granted them; he forbade them only the possession of Christian slaves who constituted the labour force for some landowners (and this is perhaps one of the reasons which caused the Jews to break away

Mantuan Jews of the Fifteenth Century with the "Sign"

from agriculture and to concentrate instead on commerce). Although the clergy were adverse, nevertheless they gained the protection of *Charlemagne*, who extending his empire to Italy, actually nominated a special magistrate to instruct them in civil and commercial rights; nor were there persecutions during the reign of the Carolingians in North/Central Italy, which favoured the formation of communities such as *Pavia* and *Verona*; nor were there grave situations in Byzantine Italy, where, for example, *Shefatiàh Amittai*, physician to *Basil I*, was actually able to obtain protection for his co-religionists; nor in Norman Italy, if one excepts the heavy taxation to which Jews were subjected. Thus, above all in the epoch of the **Ottos** (10th cent.), in the communities of Rome or Bari, Otranto or Sicily, studies flourished to such a point that the learned Italian Jews were admired all over Europe; among the famous were *Joseph Ben Gurion*, author of a chronicle known as *Josippon*; members of the Amittai family, and in the scientific field, *Shabetai Donolo of Oria*. When, however, the phenomenon of **feudalism** was propagated, the Jews found they were dependent on the fickleness of various lay and ecclesiastical feudatories and their conditions began to grow more uncertain and fluctuating. But, nevertheless, in the time of the **Crusades**, when life was fairly difficult for European Jews, persecuted by violent religious fanaticism, they

lived, even with the usual restrictions, on the whole a tranquil life, finding in Rome some defence in the Papacy, and in the South good opportunities for the diffusion of trade, developing, above all, the silk industry. Such economic development favoured Jewish settlements as well in the maritime republics which in the meantime had assumed capital importance; in *Venice*, first of all, to safeguard its own economic interests and its own commercial rights, it seemed then that Jews were forbidden to have permanent residence in the city. In the last two centuries of the Middle Ages (13th-14th), however, though in a condition of inferiority, Jews could lead a dignified life, often consulted by nobles and sovereigns for their learning and often regarded as a determining factor in the economic vicissitudes of single centres, for their ability and powers of achievement. But their existence was by now directly connected with the behaviour of the Papacy; thus in the *IV Lateran Council* (1215) Pope **Innocent III**, while maintaining certain concessions, sanctioned the laws which obliged Jews to live apart from the rest of the population and to wear a distinctive sign: a pointed hat, a red or yellow stripe on the dress, or, more commonly, a yellow circle on the left shoulder. Their condition was, however, at the same time, good in the Kingdom of Sicily under *Frederick II*, open to every cultural influence, and where, for that reason, learned Jews were admitted and welcomed with the same acclaim shown to all men of learning; difficult with the kings and popes following, even though their importance on an economic plane as ever saved them, both from the hostility of *Charles of Anjou*, who favoured the anti-Jewish sermons of the Dominicans, and from that of *Boniface VIII* (1295-1303).

In the 14th cent., following the immigration of French Jews driven from their lands, and German Jews, the Italian Jewish population grew considerably; and during the period **of the Avignon Captivity of the Papacy** (1305-77) and the Angevin government in southern Italy, while undergoing trouble and vexation, while objects of grave and infamous accusations, such as that of profaning the Host or carrying out ritual sacrifices with human blood, they managed to establish themselves in new centres, trading, progressing in the arts, excelling in medicine, defended from the violence of the people and forced conversion. On the other hand, in North Italy where there was no united government, it was above all commercial relations with the various cities that conditioned the life of Jews; thus they had the chance of establishing themselves for a set time in *Venice*, against heavy payments, and were able to found a rich community in *Padua*, too, where they were engaged in trade and banking activities. In all the period, however, they could pursue various activities; they were agricultural proprietors in the south, able weavers and dyers, practised in all operations connected with marine commerce, in the north; they shone in biblical and talmudic studies; in liturgic and profane poetry, and there were famous names such as Jeshajà da Trani, Beniamino 'Anau da Roma, Calonimos ben Calonimos from Provence but living in Italy, and best known of all, Immanuel Romano, poet and imitator of Dante.

Rome. The Portico of Octavia.

Venice. Museum of Jewish Art. A "milàh" of the end of the Eighteenth Century (detail).

Venice. Museum of Jewish Art. A "milàh" of the end of the Eighteenth Century.

During **Humanism** and **the early Renaissance** conditions of life for the Jews changed fairly noticeably: one witnesses, in fact, a definite turning point in their activities. When the Church uncompromisingly forbade their own faithful to engage in money lending at interest, it was actually the Jews who developed this activity, becoming soon, with their Pawnbrokers' Shops, sought after or disparaged depending on circumstances. The papacy, engaged upon the Great Schism, continued its contradictory policy, with anti-Jewish regulations not put into practice, and was favourable to Jews under *Martin V*, so much so that some communities thought of uniting into one single organization (*Padua, Ferrara, Bologna, etc.*) and at times with *Eugenius IV* and *Innocent VIII*. In the north the communities of *Venice* developed more and more; Jews, while compelled to make heavy contributions and wear the yellow badge, with their money-lending activities, were a positive landmark for the poorer population; in *Ferrara*, favoured by the Este policy that was fairly liberal on the whole; in *Florence*, where Jews were explicitly invited by the Medici to engage in money-lending; in *Turin, Casale and Moncalvo*, made up mostly of French immigrants.

On the other hand, in the south and in the islands the anti-Jewish laws emanating from Spain began to make themselves felt, and inasmuch as they continued to develop trade and industry, and Jews actually had their own parliament (1489), they could not in the end, **in 1492**, avoid expulsion and confiscation of goods. But meanwhile in all Italy the gravest danger came from the violent sermons preached by the Minorites and especially by **Bernardino da Feltre** who attacked the Jews on the religious plane, accusing them of ritual homicide and inciting the people against them, and on the economic plane, with the institution of Pawnshops, a real obstacle to Jewish moneylending. Notwithstanding this, studies and letters flourished more than in other epochs: among the famous were *Ovadiah da Bertinoro*, traveller and exegete, who died in Israel, *Elia del Medigo* had among his scholars in Florence *Pico della Mirandola*; *Mose da Rieti*, imitator of Dante, was a distinguished poet; while with the invention of printing, many printing houses sprang up to publish Jewish books.

But **1492** was another dramatic and decisive turning point for Italian Jews: when **Ferdinand the Catholic** issued the famous decree by which he drove all Jews out of Spain and out of the lands in its possession, the consequent arrival of refugees, and the reviving religious fanaticism provoked a veritable wave of hatred which broke upon the Jews, accused by the "Minorites" in their sermons of the most infamous actions: of poisoning wells, of ritual homicide, of spreading epidemics and similar things. They were forced to emigrate from many cities with the consequent loss or confiscation of their possessions; in many other cities, however, they were allowed to stay but were forced to live in quarters surrounded by walls and separated from the rest of the city. This was because their economic presence was by then indispensable although they could not possess real estate or engage in manual labour but just had to devote themselves to small-time peddling,

Venice. Museum of Jewish Art. A Chanukàh

Venice. Museum of Jewish Art. A parocheth. depicting the Jews in the desert

moneylending or medicine. In this way they lost their freedom even though, given the situation, segregation was not entirely a negative factor, for in that way they were defended from the violence and insults of the common people, they could find an internal unity, give themselves a unitarian constitution and respect their own traditions. Thus began that chapter in the history of the Jews in Italy that lasted for about three centuries and was the period of the **segregation in the Ghetto**. In 1516 Venice was the first to assign a quarter to the Jews, the site of the foundries ("getto" in Venetian from which the word "ghetto" derived and later extended to all the cities). Then, after the terrible **Bull of Paul IV in 1555**, the example was followed by nearly all the other cities.

Every ghetto had its synagogues, called *"Scole"*, its rabbis, its teachers, its welfare associations, and was like a little closed world, static, where ancient uses, customs and traditions remained alive, where they had a particular speech, a mixture of Jewish and various local dialects. sometimes not to be understood by unaccustomed ears, but where Jews were divided according to the rites they used in their prayers. Those most widely diffused were **three** (and still are to a great extent to-day): the "**Italian**", derived from that practised by the first Jews who came to Italy, to Rome, in the South or the islands, then emigrated to the north to form new communities: the "**Spanish**", called "Sephardic" in use among Jews coming from Spain and Portugal after the 1492 expulsion; lastly the "**German**", called "Ashkenazic", brought by the Jews who came to Italy from Central Europe, to avoid the persecutions, or by the Provencal-French, in part, following the expulsions of the 14th cent. Each major centre thus had a predominant group; the Piedmont/Lombard communities were of the German-Italian rite; those of the Veneto, firstly of German-Italian rite, then, mostly of Spanish rite; the Emilians of German-Spanish rite; Tuscans of Italian rite, with the exception of Sephardic Leghorn; Rome for a long time of Italian rite, including also the immigrants of the southern communities, then from the 15th cent. Spanish, too. Life in the ghettos was not easy: Jews were closed in a small area, compelled to live in houses which developed upwards, with danger of collapse, fires, epidemics; often derided and scorned by the common people with defamatory songs, but at least safer than elsewhere from sackings and assaults, which, however, were not entirely lacking. This did not prevent, in the long period of segregation. the flowering of letters and arts, in relation to the commercial-economic developments of cities like *Venice*, where for example Rabbi *Leon da Modena* became famous in the 17th cent.; or *Leghorn*, the best known printing centre in Italy for Jewish books; but the Jew was always considered inferior and not worthy of freedom. It was during this very troubled period that the somewhat superficial picture of the Jew as a merchant and usurer emerged: always ready to look after his own interests, always engaged in business, astute, shabbily dressed, with a hooked nose and a nasal voice. The Jew was the "odd man out" in an established society, someone to be hunted down as an infidel. Certainly the situation was not the same in every city. Apart from Leghorn which was the second largest community in Italy after Rome and which never had a ghetto, no "serraglio" was more wretched than the one in Rome where the close presence of the Pope was all-important. Meanwhile, however, in the enclosures in Venice and Florence life passed fairly peacefully, even though this peace cost the Jews dear. Nevertheless, this was the most typical period of Italian-Jewish history whose vicissitudes are still remembered in the few remaining synagogues and in the numerous books and manuscripts which were saved from being publicly burnt on the orders of the Church, or in the objects of worship, now collected in the museums of the most illustrious communities.

When, in fact, the ghettos were abolished between the 18th and 19th century, the history of the Jews in Italy began to develop in parallel lines to the vicissitudes of the nation. The hatred began to abate, if not actually to disappear; in 1782 *Joseph II of Habsburg* issued the Edict of Toleration inspired by the principles of illuminated despotism; in 1791 revolutionary France conceded equal rights to Jews. 1848 was, however, the year of real emancipation; King *Carlo Alberto* proclaimed it in his statute, while the Jews participated actively in the *'Risorgimento'* movement, often making a heroic contribution of blood for the freedom of the nation of their adoption; up to 1870, when Rome, too, was freed, and the gates of its ghetto finally broken down.

From then the Jew was a citizen like every other, with equal rights and duties; some filled high positions in the State, others emerged in the various fields of economics and learning. Imposing synagogues rose in Florence (1882), Rome (1904), Turin, Trieste, almost a symbol of the regained freedom, and despite the dangers of assimilation, the various communities remained united and bound to tradition until the new and most tragic wave of hatred and Nazi persecution, from which once again, notwithstanding the thousands of victims, Italian Jewry succeeded in saving itself and reflourishing.

Venice. Square of the New Ghetto (detail)

THE SYNAGOGUE

Throughout the centuries the development of Jewish art has been intimately linked on the one side with the vicissitudes and wanderings of the people, on the other with tradition and religious exigencies; these factors have always conditioned the forms and various expressions of art.

So long as the Temple of Jerusalem existed, it was the one supreme symbol, even from architectonic and decorative viewpoints, of every artistic expression, but after its destruction (70 A. D.) and the subsequent Dispersion, Jewish art split up into various forms, even though the one architectonic symbol of the Jews was the **Synagogue**.

This came into being firstly as an institution beside the Temple, and as a meeting place of the single communities. The synagogue gained great importance under the *Pharisaical movement*. Pharisaism being, in fact, a popular movement which laid particular stress upon the study of the oral laws, it added to the value of the places where the people might meet for such studies. Once the Temple was destroyed, it was again the Pharisees who extended to the Synagogue its existing prerogative of Sanctity, making it not only a meeting place for purposes of study, but also a house of prayer, and making it the only central institution of the Community, especially in the Dispersion.

Thus, it assumed in ancient times and maintained for centuries, **three** special **functions**; firstly, **Beth ha Keneseth**, meeting house and house of prayer, the place where every Jew used to say his own prayers or listen to those of a *hazan* (officiating cantor), and where he performed ritual ablutions; for this purpose, often annexed to or incorporated in the building was a place for the bath (Mikvah) with a marble bath or impluvium; secondly it was **Beth Midrash**, house of study, where one met to study, under the guidance of a rabbi the Torah (Teaching) or to make decisions in the small tribunal which was sometimes found in a small place built for this, on points of ritual; these two functions explain the presence of many places annexed to the hall of worship itself; finally, the synagogue performed a **social function**, becoming the centre of the daily life and often the commercial life of the community, to transact business and often to hold markets there. The Jews there were divided into corporations, that is to say 'Schools' (**Scole**) and even when the term changed in meaning, it was the only one by which the temples were known up to later times, particularly in Italy (for example, the Spanish School in Venice, the Catalan School in Rome). Only in recent times, since the Emancipation, when the Synagogue lost many of its functions, remaining only the hall of prayer, did it assume the unique name of Temple (for example: The Greater Temple in Rome, The Temple in Florence).

The building of synagogues and their decoration with objects of worship and sacred vestments was, therefore, the only expression of Jewish art, the Jew not being able to express himself freely in painting or sculpture of the human figure, following the Ninth Commandment. It was thus a purely religious art, for which reason Jews lack an artistic tradition of their own. In building synagogues they sometimes adopted the architectonic features of the countries where they found themselves, seeking always, however, to put in evidence a sign or structure recalling the Temple at Jerusalem, adapting such forms to their own feelings and exigencies, thus avoiding a passive or reflected imitation. In the days when they endured the bitterest hatred, then they sought to make these buildings of the cult inconspicuous externally, often taking the trouble to confuse them with surrounding buildings to avoid acts of violence, and so as not to hurt people's feelings.

Such expedients and characteristics are to be encountered even more noticeably in the Middle Ages and at the time of the ghettos, when, building synagogues, they always adopted fairly linear spatial solutions, and often the hall of worship resembled a simple rectangular room, including the two fundamental elements: the **Aron** or Holy Ark, turned towards the East, and containing the Holy Scrolls of the Torah (Sephardim) which are extracted and read at particular weekly religious functions, on Saturdays or during festivities; and the **Bimah** or pulpit of the officiant from which the hazan (cantor) recites the prayers or the rabbi preaches his sermons. But as if in compensation for such limitations, they always wanted, in every epoch, to make the House of Worship splendid as regards interior decoration, with rich ornamentation and magnificent sacred vestments. The richest families, above all from the Sixteenth Century onwards, often gave huge donations to adorn and embellish oratories and synagogues, thus linking the name of the building (Luzzatto School in Venice, Gallico Oratory in Rome) to their own; many gave sacred objects, silver crowns for the scrolls of the Torah, pinnacles or terminals finely worked, often chiselled by the finest artists of the time; the women, with their own hands, embroidered precious drapes and curtains to place before the Holy Ark (parochioth), which they then left, under their name, to the synagogue to which they belonged, expressing in every image a typically Jewish artistic taste. Only in the era of Emancipation, almost like a sign of refound freedom, did isolated synagogal buildings begin to rise, majestic outside and in which, to avoid resemblances to Christian churches, they recall the styles of distant lands, new or little used in the cities of adoption, such as Asiatic style, Assyrian-Babylonian, Moorish, arriving finally at the most modern dictates of present day architecture.

The typological development of the synagogue understood as the central edifice of the Jewish community, above all during the Dispersion is fairly complex. A characteristic common to all the buildings is to have the side containing the **Aron** (Holy Ark) turned towards Jerusalem, site of the Temple and ideal centre of Hebraism; what differentiates them, apart from diverse interior space solutions, is actually the side turned towards Jerusalem, together with the position of the **Bimah** (pulpit), which can be in the middle of the hall or on the side opposite the Aron.

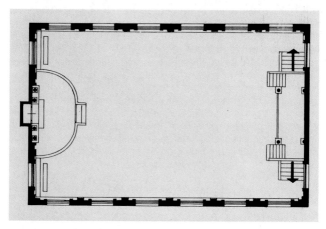

Plan of Synagogue of 3rd type (Spanish School. Venice)

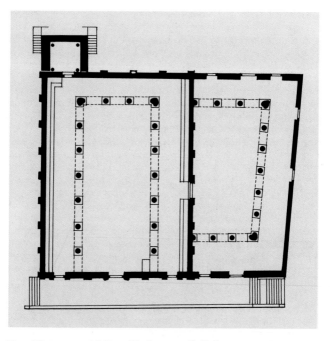

Plan of Synagogue of 1st type (Capharnaum. Galilee)

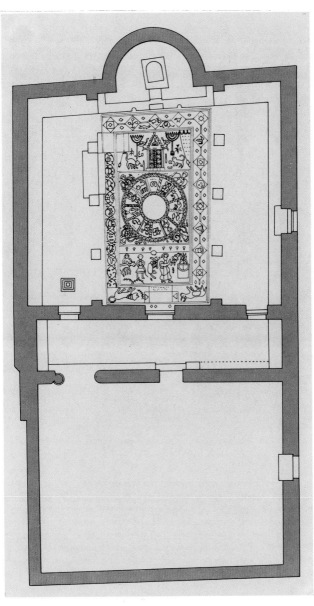

Plan of Synagogue of 2nd type (Beth Alpha. Galilee)

Leghorn. The Destroyed Synagogue. Interior (from a drawing of the Eighteenth Century)

In **the first centuries of the vulgar era three types** of synagogue could be distinguished: **a)** those going back to 2nd-3rd cent. A. D., nearly all in Galilee *(Capharnaum, Kerezeh, Kafr Bir'im)*: they have the façade turned towards Jerusalem, have a more or less regular rectangular plan, divided internally by columns, often arranged along three sides without determining a division into naves but filling the hall chessboard fashion. The façade has three entrances, the central one monumental. Along the wall run benches for the faithful, while the women perhaps used to take their places in women's galleries supported by the same columns. Inside, behind the front wall, there is a small space, surrounded by an architectonic partition, in which is found the Aron, often mobile, which puts the principal entrance out of use and compels the opening of an entrance on the long side. The hall is often flanked by a courtyard, surrounded by covered colonnades. The decoration is characteristic, mostly carved, or, if mosaic, reduced to pure geometrics. These synagogues present little origi-

co loro Loggiati e tutti gl'arredi Esteriori della med.^{che} servono ad uso di Sedili, e p. Illuminarle

Fatta a Gienna da me Me Moisè di Ioseph Del Conte in Livorno 13 Luglio

nality of structure, deriving their architectonic motives from either Syriac or Hellenistic sources.

b) those going back to the 4th-8th cent. A.D. nearly all in Galilee *(Beth Alpha, Ma'on, Cana)*; they have a longitudinal basilical plan, with apsidal end walls. The interior space is clearly divided by two rows of columns, into three naves, each of which has its own particular entrance. The façade is no longer turned towards Jerusalem, but the apsidal wall is, in which is the Aron. This has become fixed and is in a favourable position regarding the entrance, avoiding the inconvenience of the synagogues of the first type. The Bimah was probably in the centre of the hall, or backed by a central pillar. Characteristic of these synagogues are the splendid mosaic pavements with animal and human figures, often of a symbolic value, which, following the reform of *Rabbi Abun* (4th cent.) even Jews might, within certain limitations, represent in their decorations.

c) Those which rose in the same period as the foregoing and are to be found almost everywhere *(Doura Europos, Priene, Eshtemoa')*: the type commonly called *'Broadhouse'* which has a mostly rectangular plan, with the fundamental characteristic of not having internal columns which can determine any division of the space. One of the long sides is turned towards Jerusalem for which reason the Aron rests against it. The entrance is on the side opposite the Aron, or on a short side. The position of the Bimah is, on the other hand, quite variable. The hall is nearly always preceded by a courtyard and presents various types of decoration, frescoes on the walls, representing stories taken from the Bible, and mosaic pavements.

In following centuries, the typology of the synagogue went towards less elaborate and precious, but more original forms. Thus, in the **Middle Ages**, among the various solutions presented one can distinguish **two principal types**, at least, so far as regards the European edifices:

a) The type with two naves, determined by a row of columns in the middle, in which the Aron is on the end wall and the Bimah usually presents the characteristic of being placed near the central columns.

b) The so-called "vaulted" type, simpler in its space solution, elongated in form, with the Aron either on the short side or halfway down the long side and the Bimah opposite this, but often in the centre of the hall.

These solutions, rather unusual in Western architecture, especially for places of worship, were chosen specially to avoid confusion with Christian churches. For the same reason an ostentatious decoration was avoided, although not entirely lacking, as, for example, at *Prague*, or in the famous synagogue at *Worms*, elements which embellished the surroundings.

Among the ancient and medieval solutions, possibly the so-called *"Broadhouse"* type presents the simplest and most original of the Hebraic schemes. It was continued through the centuries with various modifications which brought the Aron and the entrance, facing each other, on the short sides, reaching its most mature phase in the greatest synagogues of the Italian **Renaissance**. Almost all the ancient synagogues of North Italy, and Venice in particular, go back in fact to this empty hall enclosing a still, motionless space, a symbol almost of the motionless, eternal presence of God, where the two most important points, the Aron and the Bimah, the seat of the word of God and that of man appealing to Him, are ideally linked by a double row of benches running along the walls.

Venice, however, presents a solution apart, even in the most widely diffused scheme. All the Venetian synagogues, in fact, present common characteristics which differentiate them from other buildings. Except tor the two Sephardic Schools, they are inserted in previously inhabited buildings or houses, that is to say without being specific buildings in themselves. They are always scarcely noticeable from the outside, so as not to be recognized, but very rich internally. Therefore the true hall of prayer is always on the second floor and never on the ground floor; here instead there is a large entrance hall as in the Levantine and Spanish Schools, which was possibly used for meetings or as a waiting room, since it was furnished with benches along the walls; this hall was often flanked by rooms for various other uses. Sometimes, in the oldest synagogues, the hall of worship is preceded by a small vestibule on the upper floor. Thus, the use of the stairs is typical. The hall of worship always has a women's gallery, either elliptical, inserted in the plan of the hall, or on one side only, above the entrances. The Aron is nearly always a complex structure, projecting slightly from the wall, while the Bimah is always raised and very ornate, as is the ceiling. Naturally, Venice became an example often followed, though with multiform variations, by many other communities, especially in Northern Italy and in particular in the Veneto.

To these traditional characteristics, even in the extreme variety of solutions, Jewry has remained faithful, save for some exceptions (such as the great Synagogue of Leghorn, now destroyed), up to the **time of the emancipation**. When, in fact, synagogues could rise anew as edifices to themselves apart, they assumed the strangest and most exotic typological schemes, composite schemes which often blended together styles of varying origins, as in the synagogue at *Rome*, of Assyrian-Babylonian inspiration, or that in *Florence*, clearly Moorish in type; or which, in the joy of refound freedom, employed contemporary ideas, even following the most daring suggestions of modern architecture, as in the contemporary synagogue in *Leghorn*.

Venice. The New Ghetto. Exterior

VENICE

Synagogues:	Ghetto Vecchio (The Old Ghetto) Small square of the Schools
	Ghetto Nuovo (The New Ghetto) Square of the New Ghetto
Museum:	Square of the New Ghetto Tel. 041.715359
Community Offices:	Ghetto Vecchio 1188 (The Old Ghetto) Tel. 041.715012
Kashèr Restaurant:	c/o Jewish Home of Rest Ghetto Nuovo 2874 (The New Ghetto) Tel. 041.716002
Kashèr Cafeteria / Bookshop:	Campo di Ghetto Nuovo Tel. 041.715359 - Fax 041.723007

THE JEWS IN VENICE

At the end of the 11th cent. Beniamino da Tudela, the learned Spanish merchant, made a long tour exploring the most important Italian-Jewish communities and left a valuable written report. Among the cities named, Venice, and the cities of north-east Italy in general, have no appreciable part, a sign that, at least up to that time, the Jewish community in the lagoon city was insignificant. This does not remove the fact, however, that Jewish settlements in or near the Veneto have been heard of from the most remote times; archaelogical remains and reliable testimonies indicate the presence of Jews in **Aquileia, Grado, Concordia** at least from the 4th-5th cent. A.D. but it was always difficult for Jews to live in the city. In fact, Venice, in its phase of economic growth, when it was on the way to becoming the most important trading centre for exchanges with the East, viewed the mercantile activity of the Jews as a competition to be feared, so much so that many times during the 10th cent. the Senate forbade Venetian ships to carry Jews or Jewish goods. It seems that at that time only groups of "German" Jews from Central Europe found somewhere to live in centres near Venice, forming the first consistent nucleus of the future community. As small traders, they did not interfere in port activities. But in the 11th and 12th cent. when Venice had become the most important, if not the only trading centre in touch with the Levant, the city, again for economic reasons, had to allow the merchants with whom it came in contact to live in the Lagoon, to open depots, offices and warehouses, and certainly Jewish merchants had their place there as well. However, in many ways those centuries still remain full of unanswered questions - on the basis of recent research it seems certain that Venice never conceded permanent residence to Jews in the city: all the documents previously produced to witness such a presence, have been proved groundless either because they are to be attributed to later periods or because they refer to cities other than Venice. The situation barely changed either in the 14th and 15th cent. During that period there was a decisive turning-point in the history of the Jews in Italy: pawnbrokers' shops came into being, an activity forbidden to Christians but which the Jews, although under particular conditions, were called on to carry out.

Jews could then be seen migrating into Northern Italy, "Germans" coming from the north and for the most part "Italians" coming from Central/Southern Italy: thus groups of money-lenders were formed around Venice in **Padua, Treviso, Bassano, Conegliano Veneto.** They only came as far as nearby **Mestre** however, since they could not come into the city of Venice which jealously conserved its own autonomy.

Indeed, only once did the Republic, under the "condotta" system, grant official residence in the city centre to Jewish money-lenders from Mestre. That was when the Republic, after the Chioggia war, found itself in economic difficulties and needed ready money to overcome them. For fifteen years therefore, from 1382 to 1397, the

"German" Jews lived in the city. This was certainly not just a favour granted to the Jews but a convenience and help to the poor of the Republic who could turn to these banks in case of need. These banks came under the strict control of a special magistracy, the *Sopraconsoli*, which levied precise taxes. Without doubt this was the first stable nucleus of the future great community, even if the right of residence was, for almost a century, always uncertain: in fact, while on the one hand a piece of land at San Nicolò on the Lido was granted for use as a Jewish cemetery in 1386, on the other, in 1397 the discovery of a long series of irregularities in the administration of the banks forced the Great Council to revoke the "condotta" and banish the Jews from the city. In this way a very uncertain and difficult period began for the "Venetian" Jewish population, but the anti-Jewish regulations were never drastic; they were compelled to wear the distinguishing badge (a yellow circle or a red felt hat) but the expulsion decree was soon changed into a residence permit limited to a maximum of fifteen consecutive days (one day's absence permitted a stay of another fourteen days); they were forbidden to possess real estate, but commerce could continue to develop; no rigorous means were ever employed and at least two quarters continued to be inhabited by Jews.

In this context, there is no justification for the deeply-rooted tradition that makes the Giudecca island (called **Spinalunga** until 1254) take its name, as has happened in other cities, from the permanent presence of Jews there: no document can prove this hypothesis. At the same time, there is no certainty that the island's name derives from the Venetian "iudegà" (meaning judged).

This situation continued until, in the second half of the Fifteenth Century, the Council of Ten, also on the advice of Cardinal Bessarion, adopted a freer attitude towards the Jews, provided they subjected themselves to controls, wore the distinguishing badge and did not attempt to acquire real estate. Thus, while their religious brothers resident in the three Venetias were passing through times of suffering and abuse, due in part to the violent anti-Jewish campaign conducted by the Minorites in their sermons, in part to the diffusion of Pawnshops, established in opposition to the Pawnbrokers' Bank, the Jews in Venice lived through a period which, although brief, was relatively serene, even if it cost them dear because of the heavy taxes levied by the State.

Nevertheless, Venice's Jewish population was subjected to a grave new peril in **the early 16th cen**t. The League of Cambrai, formed by the major Italian powers, had in 1509 inflicted a severe defeat on the Serenissima, creating great internal difficulties. At the same time the descent of the Lansquenets into the northern regions had spurred the Jewish residents of Treviso, Verona, Padua and Bassano to emigrate and seek refuge in the safe territory of the Lagoon. It was the right moment for the preachers to incite the people against the Jews and demand their mass expulsion. They defended themselves through their most authoritative representatives who emphasized the heavy taxes paid and the help given to the city's economy, and Venice chose a compromise solution which then became a model for many other cities: it did not expel the Jews but simply relegated them to a closed quarter, isolated from the rest of the population. After discarding the idea of the Giudecca and the island of Murano, a quarter was chosen near S. Gerolamo, the site of the new foundry (*"getto"* in Venetian) and where material was deposited in a vast square. And so in 1516 the first **Ghetto** in Italy came into being. Seven hundred Jews, mostly "Germans" but also "Italians", entered it within a short time, evacuating the few inhabitants and crowding into the existing houses. It was the less active part of the Jewish population who were forced to operate the Pawn Banks to help the poor Venetians, under the constant control of the magistrates at the *Cattaver*, committed to continually rising contributions or loans, and ably led by *Anselmo del Banco*, their recognized head. In spite of this they were soon able to organize themselves in "Universities", that is to say a small independent community with its own administration, its own Rabbi, its own synagogue: in fact the building of the great German School, the oldest and possibly the most valued in Venice, goes back to 1528-29, and

Venice. Plaque at the entry to the Old Ghetto

the Canton School to 1531-32. The other Jews, the "**levantine**" merchants, divided into "wanderers" and "residents", so important for Venetian maritime commerce and also subjected to the supervision of the *"Five Sages of Commerce"*, enjoyed a different treatment from then onwards, even though they were forced to find rooms, during their stays, in the German sector. This is shown by the splendid Levantine School which oral tradition says they founded in 1538 in the vicinity of the ghetto; in **1541** they too were taken into the ghetto, called the **Old Ghetto**, that is to say an area comprising the lanes and small squares near the New Ghetto. However, the "**Spaniards**", especially the marranos, also called *"ponentini"* after their place of origin and expelled from Spain in 1492, had been welcomed into the city after various refusals, bearing in mind the considerable economic benefits they brought to the Republic with their experience and their close association with Venetian merchants but they were only welcomed into the ghetto in 1589. They were united with the "Levantines" in the same sector of the Old Ghetto, in an ever more reduced space, forcing them to build upwards, that is to say to erect the so-called Venetian "skyscrapers". In spite of this situation, the 16th cent. was a fairly peaceful and positive period: from the point of view of commerce, because the number and prestige of the Jewish merchants, thanks above all to

Venice. The "Beth-Midràsh" of Leon da Modena

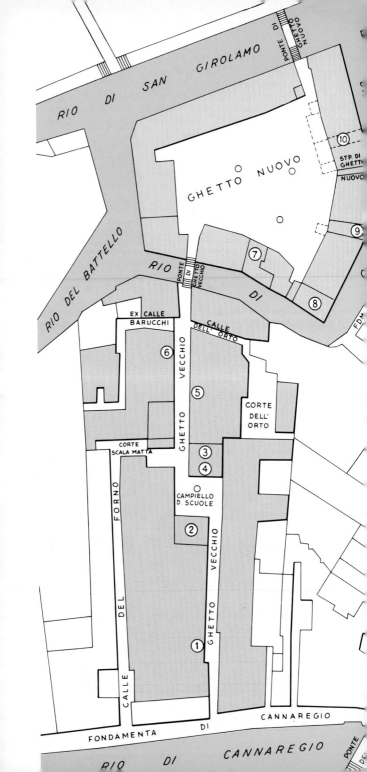

CALLE DI GHETTO NUOVISSIMO

CL. DI
GHETTO NUOVISSIMO

NUOVO

PLAN OF THE GHETTO IN VENICE

Daniele Rodriguez, noticeably increased; from an artistic point of view because at that time the other two Venetian synagogues were built, the Spanish School, which is the largest, and the Italian School; and also from a cultural point of view because in this century the diffusion of Jewish printing houses began, first of all with *Daniel Bomberg's*, where about two hundred Jewish works were published, and then the no less famous *Alvise Bragadin's* Giustinian printing house, and then the *Vendramin*, and all this could help make their lost freedom seem a less weighty burden.

However the best period for Jewish Venice, even within the above mentioned limits, was without doubt the **early 17th** cent. when economic motives once again favoured the Levantine "nation" in a particular way. The Republic was gradually losing its dominion over the Mediterranean, beginning its slow economic decline; the Venetian aristocracy, engaged in internal struggles and especially in the dispute with the Church, was transforming itself into a landed aristocracy, turning its attention towards the mainland. In this way they often left trade with the East, with all the risks it entailed, in the hands of the Jews who, because of their relations with eastern communities, were favoured in exchanges since they had safe backings and diverse wharfage. And so it was that trade in cloth, precious materials, objects of value prospered, and this brought prosperity not only to one "nation" in the Ghetto but also to the German Jews in whose shops, side by side with the usual second-hand ones, precious materials and jewels appeared, so much so that in 1629 they were also allowed to trade in wool and silk. Such conditions were immediately reflected on the cultural plane; it was the period of famous Rabbis: **Leon da Modena**, a strange and eclectic personality, equally versed in religious studies and the humanities, author of many works and propagator of culture, to whose sermons and lessons, held mostly in the Italian School, even learned non-Jewish men came; **Simone Luzzatto**, venerated for his doctrine, open to cultural exchanges, author of a small work on the condition of the Jews of his time. It was the period of no less famous poets: **Sara Copio Sullam**, a gifted poetess admired for her beauty and culture, held one of the most famous literary salons in the Ghetto, which was frequented by learned men and aristocrats, drawn there by her fame; the period which saw the flourishing of the Jewish press and the diffusion of works by Jewish authors who published in Venice: *Deborah Ascarelli*, *Angelo Alatrini*, etc. and not even the plague which in 1630 struck a great part of Italy, and decimated the population, had disastrous effects. Many Jews fled, seeking safety elsewhere; the port remained closed for a year, arresting economic development; but immediately afterwards there was a rapid recovery, to such an extent that the influx of Jews increased and towards the middle of the century it seems there were about five thousand in the Ghetto.

This was, however, a unique moment, destined never to be repeated; for from the *second half of the Century,* the crisis and decadence of the Republic began to make itself felt also on the dwellers in the "chazer" (as the Ghetto was called in Venetian-Jewish jargon). In

Venice. Alley of the Old Ghetto

fact, to cope with the growing Turkish preponderance, Venice had to seek more and more funds and naturally the tributes demanded from the Jews increased, just as sums given as loans to the State coffers increased. Economic difficulties, the insecurity of wharves in the East, forced many "Levantines" and "Ponentini" to leave Venice for more favourable spots. Moreover, the crisis also hit the lower ranks of the population, and above all the famous banks in the Ghetto, which were three at the beginning of the century, the "red", the "green" and the "black" (so called after the colour of the receipts they issued), had to seek subsidies from the various Jewish "nations" to keep themselves in business.

The situation worsened gradually in the course of the **18th cent.** economically speaking, while the Jews, from a psychological point of view continued to live in fairly favourable conditions. Economically the money-lenders became more and more uneasy; they resorted to loans from foreign communities, even though the community itself acted as guarantor, but, in 1737, they could no longer face up to their debts and they were declared insolvent. Only certain large families prospered, concentrating into the hands of a few the maritime agencies and the spinning factories; thus the number of Jewish shipowners increased, but so also did the number of pedlars, of old-clothes sellers, of small tailors, in short of the poor. However, a greater sense of tolerance seemed to surround the inhabitants of the Ghetto; the custom of wearing the distinguishing badge was allowed to elapse; the Venetians went on consulting Jewish doctors. Jewish culture became the object of greater veneration; the same Pawn Banks could slowly pay their debts and thus remain in business until the first years of the following century. Only in the last thirty years, when the Republic was living its last days, did new restrictions, now more cruel, now more moderate, fall upon the "Judeans" with the "77 condotta". Thus the minor communities of the Veneto little by little fell into ruin, such as **Conegliano, Castelfranco, Vittorio Veneto,** until they became extinct; the Jewish population decreased more and more until by the end of the century it was reduced to little more than 1,600 people.

These were the Jews who were present in **1797** at the **opening of the Ghetto** and the elimination of the gates. The French, bearers of the word of freedom and equality, acknowledged such rights also to the Jews. The Ghetto assumed the name of *"District of the Union"* and its dwellers were free citizens. Even the impositions placed upon them by Austria, to whom Napoleon had sold Venice under the Treaty of Campoformio, did not weigh upon their existence in any determinative way, and though living in wretched conditions, Jews could take part in the ordinary life of the city. Such a situation, moreover, favoured the immigration into Venice of many fellow-Jews who found themselves in difficult conditions in other parts of Italy, and it was above all Roman Jews who, to escape the wretchedness of papal Rome, came to swell the community. Thus while always remaining in the Ghetto, attached to their own traditions and cults, in a little world by now spatially open but sentimentally closed within the links with their own past, the Jews of the **age of emancipation** participated in the Risorgimento movement with a substantial contribution of works and of blood. When, in 1848, *Daniele Manin* succeeded in giving life to the Veneto Republic, two Jews actually formed part of the government, one *Isacco Pesaro*, as Minister of Finance, and, also as a minister, *Leone Pincherle*. Then, in 1866, after the annexation of Venice to Italy, even *Vittorio Emanuele II* acknowledged equal rights.

Many wealthy families went to live in mansions in the city, while only the poorest families remained in the Ghetto and it was actually among the latter, who were much more linked to material and daily needs, much nearer sentimentally to tradition, that the typical Judean-Venetian jargon was continued. It had spread over a long period and reflected a mentality and a way of life now irretrievable. The tensions of the second half of the 19th cent. and, worst of all, of the First World War, fell on them: many Jews were compelled to leave the city; the community saw its numbers drop perceptibly. The Nazi persecution, which did not spare the elderly, nor women nor children, killed or deported into extermination camps almost a fifth of the Venetian Jews and brought this parabola to a tragic close. It was the last dramatic moment in an existence which, if compared with the tribulations endured by Jews in other parts of Italy, might seem peaceful on the whole. Afterwards, the Jewish community began to live again; on their return, in the euphoria of liberation, when joy recalled all those dispersed back around the old centre of the Ghetto, new institutions and associations were created; more than a thousand members participated actively in community life, dedicating themselves at the same time to all trades and professions, living in various quarters of the city but ideally united around a single centre: those lanes and those synagogues which are a unique example in the world and remain the memory of a great past.

Let us now visit the Ghetto, the Synagogues and the Museum which collects the most precious religious objects of the old community, following an itinerary that does not correspond to chronological exigencies, leading us from the oldest parts to those nearer to us, but one less difficult for the tourist.

THE GHETTO

Among the great Jewish communities of the past, Venice is the only one to possess the old Ghetto almost unchanged. Here for centuries, the Jews lived their troubled life, closed within a particular world, with their worship, their traditions, their schools; almost a little state in itself. Gathered around the five major synagogues, which had a definite social function, with their rabbis and their institutions, they dedicated themselves to various trades: tailors, shoemakers, hawkers, the poorest; money-lenders or shipbuilders, the richest. During the day they could circulate freely in the city, but at

sunset, they all returned to the Ghetto where, during the night, the guards, paid by the Jews themselves, watched over the entrances and the canals, and from which they could leave only at dawn.

In the morning some trumpet blasts announced that it was the hour of the ceremony; in the synagogue, where everyone had his own habitual place, apart from the prayers, they listened to the rabbis' sermons, on biblical topics or questions of the day, and it was not rare that non-Jewish friars and learned folk also attended. Then each went to his own job, the young to the religious schools (*Yeshivoth*) where the best teachers taught and the *Midrashim* (rabbinical seminaries), of which one can still see the famous one where *Leon da Modena* gave lessons and, facing it, a later one of *Giacobbe Vivante*. If it were a festival day, and above all *Purim* (Feast of Lots), a festival of joy, it was not rare to see in the Ghetto many Christians who would come to take part in the games and theatre performances.

For the whole day there was, therefore, a continuous animation in the streets, chatting and often gossip in the typical jargon, made up of Venetian, Spanish and Italian elements mixed with Jewish expressions; it was, in short, a little world, with its typical figures, where everybody knew everything about everyone, where there were little disputes, malicious comments, little personal jealousies, but where basically they were all united, linked by a common destiny. In the evening, when the gates of the Ghetto were closed and the guards checked the entrances, all returned to their own homes, tiny and insufficient to hold a huge population, built upwards for lack of space, leaning one against another, with the continual danger of collapse, of fires and of the diffusion of epidemics. This was the life of the Jews of the Ghetto when, although compelled to wear the yellow badge, obliged to pay heavy tributes, without being able to enjoy the most elementary rights enjoyed by the rest of the population, without being able to possess houses or real estate, without being able to follow noble professions or arts, they could nevertheless live for centuries, sheltered from violence and assaults, such as happened in other cities, in positive collaboration with the Venetians who were never openly hostile.

The Ghetto stands at the point of confluence of three parishes: the **Old Ghetto**, which dates from **1541**, belongs to S. Geremia; the **New Ghetto**, which was the first the Jews entered in **1516**, to S. Gerolamo; the **Newest Ghetto**, added in **1633** to the present-day S. Alvise. Before the Jews were confined there, that land was the "*getto*", that is to say the foundry for the mortars of the Republic and it was used until the 14th cent. It was then abandoned and was a closed area from which, across a bridge and through a door, one arrived in a sector where the debris of the furnaces was accumulated. The Jews occupied it in three days, taking over the existing houses and quickly adapting them to their own needs.

Still today one arrives at the Old Ghetto from the Fondamenta di Cannaregio, through a **portico**: on the sides of it are still to be seen the signs of the gates which were closed at night, and the two

◄ Venice. The Old Ghetto. Little Square of the Schools

little windows, now walled up, from which watched the guards. It comes out into a long alley which receives very little sunlight (**Calle di Ghetto Vecchio**). On either side are typical tall houses which seem to choke it. In spite of many restorations, it preserves its old atmosphere; in 1541 "Levantines" and "Ponentini" were confined here: a tablet on the left a little beyond the portico, today barely legible, recalls that it was forbidden to swear, forbidden for any converted Jew to associate with the Ghetto, it indicates the possible penalties and the reward for every accusation (1704). The now renovated building standing to the left, just past the portico, used to house the *Talmud Torah* (religious school) of the *"Ponentini"*.

The long alley leads to the **Campiello delle Scuole**, a large space on which face the *Spanish School* and the *Levantine School*, from which it takes its name. Perfectly quadrangular originally, it lost its symmetry with the enlarging of the Levantine School: in fact, the well is no longer in the centre and the white ornamental strip on the paving seems interrupted. The east and west sides comprise typical old houses, disproportionately tall with respect to the square (the skyscrapers), while the south side is occupied by tne Spanish School and the north by the Levantine School.

Venice. Spanish School, Entrance

THE SPANISH SCHOOL

This is the largest of the Venetian synagogues and perhaps the only one in the world to have functioned uninterruptedly from its foundation until the present day. Built in the second half of the 16th century (1555 or 1584) by the Spaniards and possibly by marranos landed in Venice, it underwent extensive restoration in 1635 which an undocumented tradition attributes to *Baldassare Longhena*, the great Venetian architect, and later, towards the end of the 19th century, without, however, losing its characteristics of solemn imposing simplicity. A separate building, it is barely noticeable from the **out-**

side, as was the custom, where only the huge, symmetrically arranged, arched windows distinguish it from a common dwelling. On the façade now, however, is a tablet in memory of the two hundred Venetian Jews deported to Nazi extermination camps during the last war. **The entrance** is on the long side, through a large wooden portal finely decorated with geometric elements in high relief, very similar in its classical composition to the portal of the Levantine School. On the arch is the following inscription: *"Blessed are they who live in Thy house, who praise Thee unceasingly"*.

The quadrangular **entrance hall** is to a great extent covered on the side walls, with commemorative tablets of well-known exponents of the Venetian Jewish community of the past, while on the short side, opposite the entrance, is a tablet in memory of the Venetians deported in 1943-44 and access to the women's gallery. The left side is flanked by a small hall of worship, an elongated rectangle, with a fine example of *Aron* opposite the entrance, that, in time past, acted also as a study hall (*Midràsh*); on the right side instead, is the stair leading to the upper storey, that is to the true and proper hall of worship. It is divided into two branches, producing an effect of serene grandeur and giving access to the hall by two entrances placed on the short side, beside the primitive *Bimah*.

The hall of worship is an elongated rectangle with the Aron and the Bimah on the short sides, but ideally united to each other by wooden benches which run along the walls and by wooden panelling on the walls themselves which goes up to the height of the windows. The benches for the faithful are placed parallel to the long sides, leaving a large empty space in the centre characteristic of all Venetian synagogues. The floor is decorated soberly with white and grey tiles arranged geometrically to form quadrangular figures. The ceiling is finely adorned with very high reliefs in wood and stucco, with a large lamp in the centre. The hall was restored, in the 17th century, and is now a fine example of early Venetian baroque, with the polychromy of its marbles and imitation marbles and the columned decoration of the balustrade of the women's gallery. Perhaps the hand of **Longhena** can be recognized in the partitions with pilaster strips on the wall, in the sober expanse of the huge windows which repeat the arched motif of the Aron and of the portal, in the balustrade with wooden columns decorating the elliptical women's gallery, similar to the one in the German School and finally in the decoration of the Aron itself.

The Aron is decorated by a spacious classical-Baroque structure, surrounded by a semicircular arch supported by pilasters, on which one reads: *"Know before Whom thou standest"*. Four columns in black streaked marble, resting on supports. with Corinthian capitals and surmounted by a pediment enclose the Sacred Ark on whose doors, apart from the Ten Commandments is a verse from the Psalms *"I have placed God before me"* and a date, 1755. Upon it, within a semicircular element are the Tables of the Law. In the large space defined by a semicircular wooden balustrade surrounding the Aron, the platform reached by two steps was inserted during

Venice. Spanish School. Interior with Aron

the restorations of the last century. Here stands the reading desk of the officiant who used, previously, to recite the prayers from the raised gallery on the side opposite the Aron. Above the platform a small tablet records that halfway through the last century an Austrian bomb struck the synagogue on the eve of the Jewish New Year, (Rosh ha Shanah) 5609, *but 'had mercy on it'*.

The Bimah consists of a pulpit, crowned by two columns with Corinthian capitals, which can be reached by means of two lateral stairways: a design which is found in all Venetian synagogues

although with variations. The wooden structure with columns and geometric decorations dates from the rather mediocre 19th century restoration. Built to contain a small organ, donated by one of the faithful and to accomodate the choir section, it has recently been removed.

Precisely because of these modifications, the hall still preserves its early splendour, often serving as the Community's only synagogue. Coming out of the Spanish School and crossing the little square, one finds immediately

Venice. The Spanish School. The Bimah (once the choir)

THE LEVANTINE SCHOOL

This is certainly the most characteristic synagogue in Venice, the most noticeable and ornate inside and out, not inserted in pre-existing buildings, but an edifice in itself.

Oral tradition has it that it was founded in 1538 by the "Levantines" when they still lived free in the surroundings before being closed within the Ghetto. It was restored on various occasions, in the following century and during the last. Some think that they can recognize the hand of Baldassare Longhena or of his school in the restorations, and in particular in the external ones.

The principal façade is a model of composite harmony; above a high ashlar plinth, it seems to be divided longitudinally in three by a series of square windows, by four wide arched windows and by corresponding elliptical openings above, all the elements marked by geometrical frames in low relief; the first on the left is today substituted by a tablet in memory of the Jews who fell in the First World War. The entrance was through the wide wooden portal, similar to that of the Spanish School, decorated by geometrical figures in high relief; now this is closed, or gives access to the small Luzzatto school which in the last century was set up in a section of the entrance hall. The short side repeats exactly the composite scheme of the façade, but above the portal, which now constitutes the true entrance, is a characteristic projection of the Bimah; a semi-hexagonal niche, with a large window to each side and a typical shell-shaped covering; imitation of a Venetian architectonic motif, possibly (the "Liagò"), which one finds also in other synagogues.

The entrance hall consists of a vast rectangular space, along whose walls run the characteristic benches. Adorned by a beautiful ceiling and a frieze in relief, it contains extremely old tablets, one of which reminds the faithful how by pity and mercy man may obtain divine good and recompense, while another, more recent, recalls the visit to Venice in 1875 of *Sir Moses Montefiore*. The following was written above the portal: *"Blessed are they who enter and they who go out"*.

The section on the right has been occupied since the last century by a small study and prayer hall, the **Luzzatto School or Yeshivàh**. Previously situated in Campo di Ghetto Nuovo, its fittings have here been adapted to an elongated rectangular hall with an entrance on the long side: the wooden *Aron*, framed in columns on a plinth and surrounded by a balustrade, is on the short side, facing the *Bimah*, steps above the level of the hall. Benches run along the walls while the floor had the usual geometric elements. Various poems in praise of God adorn the walls, the initials of whose verses form the name *Elia Aron Chazàq*. On the left side of the entrance hall, however, opens up the stairway (after the first steps one sees the tablet with the acrostic of the name of God, which is also divided into two ramps, giving two accesses into the long side of the hall of worship.

The Hall of Worship has a transversal plan with the *Aron* and the *Bimah* on the short side and entrances flanking them. The characteristic benches along the walls, the seats parallel to the long sides, leaving the customary empty space in the centre, the wonderful ceiling decorated with geometrical wood carving and gilding in late Baroque style, the decoration of the walls where wooden frames and damask panels alternate between the windows, the women's gallery on the long entrance side, erstwhile closed by carved gratings make up a splendid surround for the two principal points of the Synagogue, giving a sense of austerity and stern meditation. The decorative complex is possibly the work of *Andrea Brustolon*, noted wood sculptor who worked here towards the end of the 17th cent. creating a perfect fusion of Jewish art and Venetian tradition.

Venice. Luzzato School and Levantine School

Venice. Levantine School. The Aron

Venice. Levantine School. The Bimah

The entrance doors present marble carvings in two colours: on the arches are verses from the Bible (near the Aron) *"How worthy of respect is this place, it is none other than the House of God"*; (near the Bimah) *"Open unto me the Door of Justice whereby I will enter and praise God"* and *"This is the Door of the Lord, here enter the Jusf"*.

The Aron, on whose doors the Ten Commandments are inscribed, is framed by a structure very similar to that of the Spanish School even if it is less wide due to the restricted space; a wide arch encloses a shrine made up of four streaked Corinthian columns on four high bases preceded by four steps and crowned by a tympanum. The following gold wording stands out on a black background above the Aron: *"I bow my head in the House of Thy Holiness and render thanks to Thy name"*, and in a small frame: *"Know before whom thou standest"*. The whole is preceded by a fine marble balustrade with polychrome ornaments and small columns, closed centrally by a brass gate which the inscription says was donated *"by Rabbi Menachem di Maimon Vivante"*. But the element of greatest value is without doubt the **Bimah**; the most ornate structure in which one can best recognize the hand of Brustolon in the multitudinous carvings and in the wooden sculpture. Above a high plinth, decorated with geometric and floral motifs and surrounded by two wide curving stairways of twelve steps, decorated by columns that effectively outline it, the pulpit appears framed by two heavily decorated twisted columns, which possibly recall those of Solomon's Temple, and by a severe architrave whose decoration immediately joins that of the ceiling. A semi-hexangonal apse enriches the background (the shrine which projects on the short external side), with a wide arched window to each side and an umbrella shaped bowl, embellished in its six festoons by geometric motifs in relief. The structure re-echoes certain other Venetian pulpits but it is the most imposing and admired of them all.

Leaving the Levantine School, facing the entrance is a small open space, once called **"Corte Scalamatta"** which leads to a narrow alley (Calle Mocato, now closed) and to the still open **Calle del Forno**, so-called because, half-way down one finds, still in active use today, the oven for the preparation of the unleavened bread (*mazàh*) and of the traditional sweets for *Pésach* (Easter). In this space is still a typical "skyscraper", called *"Scale Matte"*, possibly from the name of a family *Calamatta*, which once lived here, or for its dark and tortuous stairs. To the right, instead, one proceeds by the other **Calle di Ghetto Vecchio**. Nearly all the buildings have undergone recent restorations but one can still recognize: to the right, the *Midràsh* (study hall) of **Leon da Modena**, modest, with an arched door, flanked by two windows which take up the motifs, similar, too, to the windows of the synagogue; to the left, almost facing it, the **Midrash Vivante** founded in 1853, with an entrance topped by a fine architrave. A little farther along, where nowadays are the

Venice. The Old Ghetto

offices of the Community, opens **Calle Barucchi**, which takes its name from the *Barukh* family who lived and owned houses there, while facing one, to the right, the narrow **Calle dell'Orto** leads to the internal Corte dell'Orto, typical examples of streets and squares of the Ghetto.

Across the bridge that marks the end of the Old Ghetto, one enters the **Campo di Ghetto Nuovo.** This is the first place where "German" and "Italian", Jews were confined in 1516, a huge open space, surrounded on three sides by the characteristic "skyscrapers", which, however much restored, preserve their one-time aspect, while the north side was demolished during the last century to build the Israelite Home of Rest. One can still see three fine well-heads with, on the sides, the coats of arms of Venetian procurators of the second half of the 16th cent. and the stone erected in 1866 to record the recognition of equal rights to the Jews by *Vittorio Emanuele II* . There were once in the Campo, in addition to the three "Pawn Banks", red, green and black (one of them is still indicated at number 2911), also several *Midrashim*, among which we must remember the *Canton School* in the corner under its own little dome, and many "Scole", three of which still exist. Just over the bridge, to the left, was the *Mesullamìm School*, of German rite (ashkenazic), which dates from the 17th cent. It was demolished with the building at the end of the 19th cent., but the Aron, framed by two raised marble columns, has been placed in a little oratory now in use near the Home of Rest. On the right as one enters the Square, one sees a 16th cent., classical inspired four columned arcade, the entrance to

THE ITALIAN SCHOOL

This synagogue is more modest and simple in its complex than the others, but no less austere for this. Last of the synagogues in the Ghetto, it was built in 1575 by the Jews belonging to the Italian "nation" truly the poorest and least numerous. Restorations and additions in following centuries have not changed its original aspect, which is as it appeared to the celebrated *Leon da Modena* when he used to deliver his famous addresses.

The exterior, if one excepts the porch, is, as ever, barely noticeable, blending with the nearby houses; the synagogue is, however, recognisable by the motifs of the five large arched windows which recall those of the German School and by a fine Baroque umbrella dome on a high polygonal drum, from which the windows illuminate the Bimah beneath. Above the central window is a crest with a crown, with the writing *"Holy Italian Community in the year 1575"*; beneath is a small plaque in memory of the Temple.

The entrance is through a modest portal and dark, fairly narrow stairs leading from a small room on the ground floor and from the atrium where written, in 19th cent. style: *"Humble in actions and secure in faith / Here comes every pious man to pray / And even he whose feet point elsewhere / Keeps his thoughts turned ever towards God"*, up to the small vestibule of the hall of worship, where there is a plaque in memory of *Rabbi Isacco Pacifici*; another recalls the restoration and inauguration of the synagogue in 1740 by the *"parnasim"* (superintendents) *Coen, Nizza and Osimo.*

Venice. The Italian School. Exterior

The Hall of Worship has a slightly elongated rectangular plan. The entrance is in the middle of the long side, almost forming an angle of 90° with the Aron and Bimah which face each other on the short sides. Benches run along the walls, with wood panelling rising to the height of the windows, while simple almost classical seats run parallel to the long side. Since 1700, **the women's gallery** has been inserted above the entrance, with lowered gratings which go well with the general structure, in symmetry with the quadrangular windows which admit light from the vestibule into the Hall. The ceiling is decorated in lacunars with rectangular and circular geometrical motifs. Along the walls there are 19th cent. inscriptions on a

Venice. The Italian School. The Aron

black background, with invocations to God and repeating, with the initials of the verses, the name of a certain *Avraham* for whom the son Isaac asks for peace. On the other hand the mainly sober decoration, also due to the prevalence of sombre colours, becomes rich in the two "centres" of the hall.

The Aron, which with doors carved on the outside, and engraved inside with the Ten Commandments, is the gift of *Beniamino Marina di Consiglio*; it is framed by wooden multi-element components; it is preceded by four steps, defined by a wooden balustrade with small stylized columns on which one can read: *"Gift and work of Menachem J. Guglielmi"*. It is in 19th cent. taste and is adorned

Venice. The Italian School: The Bimah

by four Corinthian columns on a high base, supporting an architrave with classical-baroque motifs, including the motif of the crown.

More noticeable is the **Bimah**; a small pulpit rising on eight finely
decorated steps but embellished by a crowning supported by columns and by an apse which opens beneath the dome, projecting by
more than two metres from the rectangle of the hall. The four
Corinthian columns, all on a high decorated plinth, are topped by an
architrave with geometrical motifs, opening in a central arch, leading
one's glance to the illuminating dome; the polygonal apse is panelled in wood up to the windows, with seats for the officiant or notable people and the walls are decorated with inscriptions on a dark

61

background, which recall the duties of the officiant. The fine centre seat is distinguished from the others by its arched crowning. The structure is 18th cent. as recorded by the writing beneath the pulpit.

Coming out of the *Italian School* and going on to the right one reaches the corner of the square where were the entrances to the Canton School and the great German School, the small *Midràsh* of the Canton School and the Fraternity of Poor Jews. Only the two major synagogues remain, but today they have only one entrance through the door of the new Museum of Jewish Art. In our itinerary the first is

THE CANTON SCHOOL

One of the most beautiful and treasured synagogues for the refinement of its decoration and the perfect harmony of its structure. It either takes its name from the Canton family, the German Jewish merchants who built it as their private oratory of the ashkenazic rite, or, less probably, from the place in which it stands ("Canton" in Venetian means "corner"). It was built in 1531-32 but was restored many times over the centuries, as can be seen from its many adorning inscriptions and tablets. It is now undergoing further restoration but nevertheless retains its primitive harmonious aspect, vying in beauty with the great German School. Confused with nearby buildings, it can be identified externally by its eccentric wooden umbrella dome rising on an octagonal drum, capable, as in the Italian School, of lighting the little apse of the Bimah. The typical motif of five windows is not, in fact, visible from the square. Its foundation date was placed on the simple arched entrance portal, while the stairs date from the 19th cent.

On the upper floor the synagogue has **two entrances**; in the first is a tablet placed by J. Fano in the last century, saying in verses: *"Unburden thyself, Oh Mortal of all evil thoughts / Moving thy feet to pray in the Temple / Think of Him to whom thou prayest and with devoted faith / Turn thy thoughts unto thy Divine Hearer"*; in the second a Proverb of Solomon announces *"Blessed is he who hearkens to me and is ready to enter my doors each day"*.

The true and proper **Hall of Worship** has an elongated rectangular plan; *Aron* and *Bimah* are on the short sides; the entrance on a long side, while on the other open five wide arched windows.The usual benches run along the walls, while the wood panelling goes up for two-thirds of the height. The seats for the faithful are arranged parallel to the long sides, with an empty space in the mid-

Venice. The Canton School. the Aron

dle where, on the floor of Venetian terrazzo rests a circular ornament with geometrical motifs. The originality of the synagogue is,
thus, in the decoration. The upper part of the walls is decorated by
a double series of panels with perforated or carved geometrical
motifs, or with biblical figures and inscriptions alluding to Moses,
the passage of the Red Sea, Jerusalem. On the entrance side such
squares are in part substituted by the gratings of the **women's gallery** which fits perfectly into the harmony of the architectonic structure. Only a festooned marble cornice decorates the ceiling, which
for the rest is painted. The tone of splendour is due, however, to the
gilding, which, as recorded by an inscription on the portal, was fin-

Venice. The Canton School. The Bimah

ished *"In the month of Elùl (August - September) 1780"*. Internally this portal is decorated with marble ornaments rising to a shell-shaped crowning, surmounted by a panel with a celebratory inscription; while a series of bronze lamps fill the space harmoniously. Particular attention has been given to the Aron and the Bimah.

The Aron, with its finely carved and gilded external doors and with the *"Kether Torah"*, (Crown of the Torah) engraved on the inside above the Ten Commandments, is preceded by four steps with the dedicatory inscription *"Gift of J. Mosheh"* in memory of a brother killed, and the name *of Mordechài Baldosa*, 1672. They are surrounded by two beautifully gilded Corinthian columns on a plinth and two pilasters which support a heavily decorated architrave. The motif is taken up in the two seats, enclosed between two columns, partly spiral, partly grooved, which flank the Aron itself, topped by square panels bearing engraved celebratory prayers for festival days. A central frame has, instead, the Tables of the Law (nowadays not visible). ·

The most original structure, however, is without doubt the **Bimah**. The little polygonal pulpit, finely decorated with geometrical reliefs, rests on a hollow, marked by five wooden steps raising it above the level of the hall. It is, however, framed in a lovely semi-elliptical arch supported by a double pair of original pierced columns whose shafts are interwined branches, which mark the end of a large polygonal apse. With two windows at the sides and wood panelling with benches along the walls, the apse is interrupted in the middle by a concave seat, crowned by a shell-shaped arch which, according to the inscription, was donated by *"Beniamino Marina di Conselve"*: on the ceiling, the opening of the dome, enclosed within coloured sections, embellishes this original space solution. A small stone at the foot, to the left, records the donation by a certain *Shelomoh* towards the building of the synagogue.

Coming out one passes various plaques reminding the faithful to do good while they live and await the mercy of God.

The composite harmony, the gilding, and above all the solution of the Aron recall, as its nearest precedent, the nearby

GREAT GERMAN SCHOOL

This is the first synagogue to be erected in the Ghetto; it was built by the old German "nation" in 1529 for the practice of the ashkenazic rite. The builder found it difficult to insert the plan of the synagogue in the already existing buildings, not being able to construct an element to itself, also because of space restrictions. Its plan thus appears slightly asymmetrical, almost trapezoidal, even though the astute decorative solution, which, despite repeated restorations, does not alter the original at all, avoids creating any feeling of disharmony in the person entering.

The synagogue is, as always, little apparent externally; only the well-known motif of five windows (three walled-up) with arches in white stone distinguish it from the surrounding dwellings.
The entrance portal is, in fact, very modest; the inscription on it: *"Great Temple of the ashkenazic rite"* appears almost identical to that under the cornice: *"Great School of the Holy Community of Germans; with the protection of God, Amen"*. Along the walls of the present stairs (restored in the 19th cent.), which lead to the hall of

Venice. The German School. The Bimah

worship, higher up, according to religious tradition, than all the other buildings and with no rooms above as in all Venetian synagogues, one can read various commemorative and celebratory inscriptions of various periods.

As observed, **the hall of worship** preserves a transverse trapezoidal plan, very asymmetrical, with Aron and Bimah on the shorter sides, opposite each other, with entrance on the long side, but near the Aron. (This lay-out dates from the 19th cent.; previously the Bimah was in the centre). The absence of columns and pilasters

Venice. The German School. The Bimah

caused the architect to employ many decorative expedients to make the hall harmonious. Along the walls run the benches and a high wood panelling; pews for the faithful, without doubt the oldest elements, run parallel to the longer sides, forming an empty space in the centre; a lovely elliptical women's gallery, adorned by a balustrade of stylized columns reproducing the motif of an octagonal lantern open at the centre of the ceiling; the identity between the circular and quadrangular decorative elements which run along the ornamental fascia of the ceiling, and, in relief, on the elliptical crown beneath the gallery; the variegated marble plaster panelling of the walls and finally the gracefulness of the Bimah combine to create an optical illusion of compositive symmetry. A contribution to all this is partially made by the circular ornamental motif in the middle of the floor of Venetian terrazzo, and the long inscriptions in gold, reproducing the Ten Commandments, which run on a fascia beneath the gallery, as if, one might think, to link together the two "focal points" of the hall.

The Aron is decorated by a complex tripartite structure, flanked by two wide windows and embellished by the gilding which restoration has at times rendered excessive. It rises, preceded by four pink marble steps, bearing the name of the donor: *"The oldest of the Zemel brothers, Rabbi Menachem Cividale"* (2nd half 17th cent.), on a decorated high plinth, framed by grooved Corinthian columns which support an architrave in Baroque style, decorated with vases and cornucopias. On the inside of the doors appear the Ten Commandments in mother-of-pearl inlay, on the outside, in very fine inlay, possibly stylized, the Tree of Life. At the sides are two candlesticks and two seats for the *"parnasim"* (superintendents) reproducing the structure and decoration of the central part. Biblical verses are written on them recalling the praise of God and wisdom. The whole imposing structure projects outwards on the short side, forming an aedicule on Rio di Ghetto Nuovo, similar to that of other Venetian synagogues.

The Bimah is singularly graceful; a polygonal aedicule, projecting strongly in respect to the end wall, it rises on a plinth, decorated with the same geometrical motif as the ceiling and on a balustrade of gilded columns: it is made up of eight slender stylized Corinthian columns which support a light cornice-architrave decorated with the same type of vases one sees above the Aron. Although not perfectly suited to the place, it nevertheless contributes to the illusion of an airy proportionality.

As we know, all synagogues were wonderfully adorned with many objects of worship, a great number of which have today been collected together in the adjoining

MUSEUM OF JEWISH ART
(The arrangements may be subject to change)

Created out of rooms near the great synagogues, after the Second World War, by the Rabbis *Toaff and Polacco*, who saw to the arrangements, in its show-cases are collected curtains, manuscripts, precious ornaments and testimonies to the religious and cultural vicissitudes of the Ghetto and of many small neighbouring communities.
Near the stairs leading to the German School are to be seen two valuable *candlesticks*, which came from Vittorio Veneto, and an 18th cent. *desk*; on the first landing of the stairs a small ornamental *fountain*, *"Gift of Moshéh Spilimbergo"*.

The first room contains two tables and seven show-cases; on their ornamental bands have been reproduced verses from Exodus.
Above the entrance door three *tasìm* (plaques) to adorn the Scrolls of the Torah, with the names of the donors (18th-19th cent.).

In the **first centre table**, above a red Renaissance *parocheth* (curtain for the Aron) with gold embroidery, and an 18th cent. *me'il* (mantle for the Scrolls) with flowers on an ivory background, are ornaments to decorate the *Sepher* (Scroll of the Torah) or which serve for the cult, all of the 17th-18th cent.: three *'ataròth* (crowns) in silver, gifts of the faithful, and one (41) particularly lovely in embossed silver with leaves and roses, given in memory of *Isacco Gentili* (end of 18th cent.); three *rimonìm* (terminals for the Sepher) in finely worked silver and gilding; various *yadòth* (indexes for reading) and *mafthachòth* (keys to the Aron).

In the **second central table**, among the other ornamental objects are: an *'atarah* (47) in silver with symbolic elements, fire, the Tables of the Law, the 12 loaves, gift of the *Luzzatto* community in the 18th cent.; two silver *rimonìm* (50) of the early 18th cent. with chiselling and floral motifs on the tiers; a silver *tas* (52) with 2 medallions (*Shadài* omnipotent) and symbols; the hands that bless, the *Menoràh* (7-branch candelabrum), the Tables of the Law (18th cent.).

In the **cases** there are mainly sacred hangings. Going towards the right: in the **first small case**, with two *me'ilìm* in brocade, are two precious Baroque style *rimonìm* (4), in chiselled and gilded silver with shelves, chains and bells.
In the **second case**, among the brocade and velvet *me'ilìm*, particularly lovely is (6) a *me'il* with gold embroidery on a violet ground, 17th cent., with the Sacred Ark in the centre and at the side a cup full of manna; nearby is a *paròcheth* (7) in velvet with embroidered silver tulips, *"Gift of Rebecca di A. Levi"* (17th cent.); a splendid group of *rimonìm* of various periods, a fine *Chanukjàh* (9-branch candelabrum) (11b) 18th cent. in bronze with floral motifs on the central branch and between the others.
In the **3rd case** apart from a *mapàh* (cover for the Sepher) in gold-embroidered red velvet (12) with the inscription *"Shadài"*, possibly 17th cent., and a *paròcheth* (15) in green velvet and gold embroidery, with the Tables of the Law in the centre (19th cent.) among the *me'ilìm* (13) one is very lovely, in yellow brocade with silk embroidery, 17th cent., with various shades of colour and a verse recalling *"the purity of the Law of God"*.
In the small **4th case**, with a *paròcheth* (19) in red velvet embroidered in gold and silver of the 17th cent. can be seen a silver jug (20), chiselled and embossed, very elegant in its 18th beauty.
In the **5th case**, between two *me'ilìm*, one with floral motifs (23) and one in floral-striped brocade (24) stands out a splendid *paròcheth* (22) on a blue ground with gold embroidery. It is entirely covered: in the upper part, between the rays of the sun which filter through the clouds, appear the Tables of the Law, resting symbolically on Mount Sinai, surrounded by a vast mountainous landscape; in the lower

Venice. Museum of Jewish Art. A "paròcheth" - The Tables of the Law on Mount Sinai

part, separated by a river, appear, on the other hand, Jerusalem with its towers and famous gates and with the structure of the Temple in the middle. Certain verses from the Psalms crown this wonderful 17th cent. work, patiently embroidered, as is written, by "Stella, wife of Isacco Perugia".

In the **6th case**, most noteworthy of all is another paròcheth (28) given, as is written on the medallion at the foot, by the Levantine Community at the beginning of the 19th cent. Possibly a copy of an earlier paròcheth, it depicts gathered together, certain moments in the sojourn of the Jews in the Desert. At the top, the Fall of Manna, with the verse: *"An omer for every man"*; at the side, the rock from which sprang water, with the words: "He opened the rock and the waters came forth"; more to the right, the quails, and the words: *"They asked and he brought quails and satisfied them with the bread of Heaven"*; finally, the tents of the Jews, of simple but good workmanship.

Among the me'ilim, notice specially (30), 17th-18th cent. in green velvet with silver embroidery, with a crest in the centre having the non-religious motifs of the lion armed with lance and shield; among the objects is a small silver citron basket (33), gift of *Salomone Aboaf de Flandes*, with neoclassic motives.

In the **7th case**, finally, together with a 17th cent. *paròcheth*, (34) are some beautiful silver *rimonìm* (35), in the shape of lanterns, with many tiers, ending in a point in the form of a vase with tiny flowers, in good Baroque taste.

Down a few steps one comes to the **2nd Room** of the Museum, which presents other religious objects, but of different types, and precious manuscripts.
Going towards the left, one sees a lovely *"Seat of the Prophet Elijah"* (53) which today serves for the ceremony of *Milàh* (circumci-

Venice. Museum of Jewish Art. The "Chuppàh" for weddings

sion), a ceremony also represented in a picture nearby (54) with words of good omen by *M. Gallico*, gift of *Gabriel Malta* at the end of the 18th cent.; in a precious lacquered gold frame one sees the participants wearing the rich Venetian garments of the 18th cent.

Following a Baroque prie-dieu and a fine shell-shaped basin with jug, in a corner is the *Aron* (56) from the synagogue of *Vittorio Veneto*; a fine Baroque work, it has a representation on top of the Tables of the Law, while in front of it is lit the *Ner Tamìd* (Perpetual Light) in finely wrought silver.

Along the left wall, beneath a somewhat modest picture by an unknown artist, representing the sacrifice of Isaac (59) some *Thiqìm* (cabinets for the Sepher), and *Kethubòth* (marriage contracts) with illuminated manuscripts and greetings.

In the centre wall, a fine *Chuppàh* (wedding canopy) (63) supported by four pilasters; in red velvet with gold decorations, early 18th cent. Under it are armchairs for the bridal pair in late 17th cent. Venetian style; the reading desk for the officiant, in walnut, of the same period; a *paròcheth* in velvet and gold of a later period; this complex is used today in marriage ceremonies taking place in the Temple.

Venice. Museum of Jewish Art. Seat of the Prophet Elijah

Nearby is a splendid *Thiq* (64), cabinet for a Sepher of the 17th cent. in silvered wood; it bears, among decorations in gold, the Tables of the Law, and on top, in the central medallion, among the decorations of the crowning, the bowl and jug for the washing of hands, symbol of the Levis. It was, in fact, the gift of one, *David Levi*, and is used even today at the time of *Sukòth* (Feast of the Booths) and *Simhath Torah* (Festival of the Rejoicing of the Torah). On the right-hand wall can be seen a *Chanukjàh* (67) in silver, in the taste of the 18th cent., but possibly deriving from an earlier model.

Inside the cupboard, work of the late 18th cent., are various pieces of silverware; citron-holders; perfume containers; goblets, *rimonìm* and *'ataròth*. To be specially remembered are a *jug and basin* of the 18th cent. (71); an *'ataràh* of the 18th cent. (73) with the symbols of the hands that bless, robes, etc. in gold relief on a silver ground; *rimonìm* (74) embossed and chiselled, of 18th workmanship and an *'ataràh* of the same period (75) from Vittorio Veneto, gift of *Aron de Jehudàh* to his Temple, as is written on the band at the foot, with praises to the Torah, in the centre.

Finally, in the **circular table** in the centre of the room, on which rests the *"pignaton"* (87b), silver 18th cent. Lamp of the Levantine

Venice. The Newest Ghetto. An entrance

School, gift of *David Maurogonato*, are collected important manuscripts and sacred objects; let us note one only, the manuscript (80) on parchment, containing the *"Book of Instruction"* of *Aronne Levi of Barcelona*, published in Venice in 1523; a splendid book cover (81) in embossed silver of the 17th cent., one side bearing the *Vivante* crest, the arm with the flag, the other, the crest of *Trieste*, the stork with crown and wheatear; a pergameneous manuscript (83) finished by *Shelachiàh da Candia* in 1403; the splendid illuminated manuscript (85) on parchment, containing the five books of the Bible with commentary, finished by *Daniel di Samuel Dayan* in 1405: in the first pages the miniatures are of floral elements, strange and mythological animals certainly not traditionally Jewish.

Leaving the Museum and going to the right one reaches the **Portico** with a wooden bridge over *Rio di Ghetto Nuovo*, across which one faces a typical image of the Ghetto Nuovo; very tall houses on the canal, in typical colours, with little windows, one beside the other. Looking to one's left one can see, towards the end of the house, a projection; it is the Aron of the German School, which projects from the short side of the hall, with a small aedicule.

Turning one's back to the bridge there is, finally, on the left, the alley which leads into the **Newest Ghetto**. It was the sector added in 1633 to the two earlier ones; formed of three blocks of houses, some lovely, actually with façades reminiscent of Sansovino, two alleys crossing in a "T". The first had the houses owned by the *Treves and Vivante* families, the second was called **Calle del Porton**, because it ended with the portal and gate which the guards closed each night. Even today the signs of the gates can be seen on the jambs, as in the portico of the Ghetto Vecchio, where we began our walk, which has led us through one of the rarest testimonies to the history of the Jews in Italy.

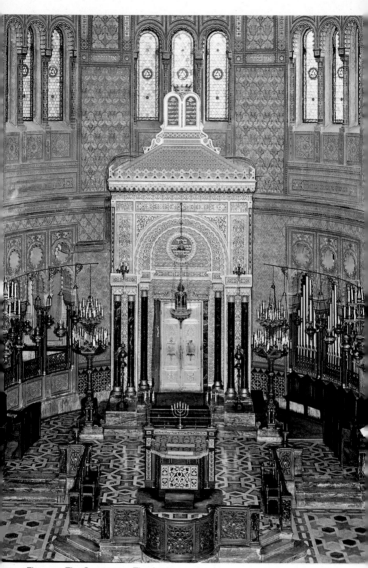

Florence. The Synagogue. The Aron

FLORENCE

Synagogue:	Via Farini, 4
Offices of the Community:	Via Farini, 4 - Tel. (055) 245252
Kashèr Restaurant: Café/Bookshop	Via Farini 2/a - Tel. 055/2480888

THE JEWS IN FLORENCE

The origins of the Jewish community in Florence are fairly late in respect to those of many other cities; one has, in fact, to wait till the 15th cent. before speaking of a consistent Jewish group in the city of the Medici. Not that there were not previously some isolated Jewish families living there, but only in the 15th cent. was there a considerable afflux of bankers and money-lenders invited by the Seigniory. Until then the Medici had forbidden loans within the city, while they flourished in various Tuscan centres and in the surroundings: in fact, between the end of the 14th and beginning of the 15th cent. many *"condotta"* or authorizations were granted, to *S. Miniato, S. Gimignano, Pisa* to the famous *Da Sinagoga* family, and, in 1406, those already existing in *Prato, Arezzo, Pistoia and Volterra* were confirmed.

In Florence, instead, only private Christian lenders were admitted and the monopoly of loans remained in their hands till **1437** when, their funds available having grown less, while the needs of the Florentines had increased, the Seigniory turned to Jewish bankers, granting them four *"condottas"* in the city. Thus was formed the nucleus of the community which, with the families of *Pisa, Tivoli, Fano,* became rich, their existence from then being linked with the Medici Seigniory, made up for the rest of wealthy bankers and merchants, led then by the most able of them all, **Cosimo I the Elder**.

Protected in that way, and above all, by **Lorenzo il Magnifico**, who on two occasions defended the community, first from the danger of expulsion, then from the uprisings provoked by the sermons of *Bernardino da Feltre,* they flourished economically and on a cultural level living a serene and prosperous life. Great moments of danger were endured, in fact, only during the period when the Medici were driven out: in 1495, when the popular government, inspired by *Gerolamo Savonarola,* decreed the expulsion of the Jews to leave room for the Pawnshops, and only a considerable loan saved the community; and in 1527 when the new elimination decreed by the republican government was avoided by the return to Florence of *Alessandro de' Medici,* after the agreement between Pope Clement VII and Charles V.

But links with the fate of one family were never very safe, and, in fact, the situation changed in the **2nd half of the 16th cent.** In the climate of the *Counter-Reformation* the papacy had issued numerous bulls against the Jews, seeking in all countries a practical application of such regulations. The Florentine Seigniory, with its new head, *Cosimo I,* did not subject to intimidations, but rather, from economic motives, at first continued to favour Jews, even in 1551 calling a group of Levantines to set up in Florence a series of commercial exchanges with the Levant. This was the first nucleus of Sephardic rite Jews to establish themselves in the Seigniory, but it was also the last positive moment in the life of the community. Only fifteen years later, in fact, **Cosimo I**, eager to obtain the title of Grand Duke from Pope *Pius V,* suppressed every scruple of conscience, and, urged by ambition, accepted anti-Jewish regulations, imposing the badge, revoking many "condottas", finally, in **1570**, insisting on **segregation in the Ghetto**. The Grand Duke's decree says this was punishment for transgressions committed and to avoid fusion with Christians. In that part of the city, now more or less the *Piazza della Repubblica*, were confined even Jews of the country-side. A few families continued to live outside near Palazzo Pitti, Cosimo's residence, in a narrow alley called *"de' Giudei"*, so that Cosimo could call on them for his own needs.

Thus began the saddest period in the history of Florentine Jews, also because, in spite of creating within the Ghetto the synagogues, the special tribunals, their own administration, these were always divided by internal hostility between the original Italian group and the more recent Spanish nucleus. Only in the **second half of the 17th** cent. was unification reached in the *"Università"* of the Jews, thus avoiding sending bad to worse. In fact, they had many economic troubles, Jews no longer being allowed to follow the wool and silk industries, nor to trade in precious objects, even though some privileged ones, but they were exceptions, had concessions for luxury goods such as brandy and tobacco. The precarious situation reduced their numbers till **in the 18th cent.** there were less than a thousand, exposed at times to the tumult of the people", but basically defended by the walls of the Ghetto.

After the Napoleonic delusion, one had to wait till 1848 to see the gates broken down. Or rather, the Ghetto itself was completely destroyed to build the new city centre. The freedom then obtained did much to favour the recovery of the whole community, which doubled the number of its members, had its own constitution, numerous fraternities, some benevolent, some of them cultural; there came a new Jewish spirit, in short, which was fully realised in **1882**, when the monumental *Great Temple*, symbol of the rebirth, was inaugurated.

But it was in the **early years of the 20th cent.** that the reawakening manifested itself even more, in the work above all of *Samuel Margulies*, a rabbi of great culture, who brought Florence almost to the point of being the ideal fulcrum of Hebraism in Italy; he it was who wanted the *Rabbinical College* in Florence; he promoted studies, founded and directed the *"Rivista Israelitica"*, having finally among his scholars two bright lights of Jewish culture, *Umberto Cassuto* and *Elia S. Artom*, who raised the prestige of Florentine Jewish learning throughout the world.

The tragedy of the War and the deportations then fell upon Florence, decimating its members, but without succeeding in extinguishing the Jewish spirit which, after the liberation, rose again, more vigorous; it restored the Temple, damaged by the War, bringing it back to its original splendour, tidied up its own institutions and above all, created and maintained the Jewish school, now bearing the name of *Nathan Cassuto*, the rabbi deported during the last War. Such vigour and zeal also allowed the Florentines to emerge into new life after the terrible **flood of November 1966,** when the

Florence. The Synagogue ►

Florence. The Synagogue. Interior

water destroyed many treasures of Jewish art, damaging the Temple, destroying part of the Old Library. The goodwill and aid of the whole world allowed them to overcome this tragic moment and to restore the Temple once again, bringing it to the state in which we can see it today

As already said, the **Ghetto of Florence** no longer exists. It rose between the present *Piazza della Repubblica* and *Piazza dell'Olio* but was completely destroyed last century to build the new city centre there. Memories of it exist, however, in certain pictures (*Signorini*, e. g.); the names of some streets or squares (*Cortile de' Bagni*, where there was the ritual bath, *Via Condotta*, etc.); in the epigraph placed on the old entrance door and which said *"The Jews were separated from union with Christians but not turned out"*; in the

hint, finally, one finds in the inscription above the arch in Piazza della Repubblica: *"The old centre of the city restored from age-long squalor to a new life"*. However, at least in one sector, the Ghetto did not present true *"squalor"*, if it is true that the urbanistic lay-out was entrusted to Bernardo Buontalenti, the famous architect, who included in the confines decorous mansions, previously inhabited by noble families. Until fairly recent times it contained oratories and synagogues of the various rites; the memory of two of them in particular, the Italian one and the Spanish one, remains, while the image of the two oratories, which sprang up outside the Ghetto, rests in two reproductions by Ottavio Levi; one was of Italian rite and ceased functioning even before the war, the other, of ashkenazic rite, was used after the war by a group of German Jews who had found refuge in Florence. They were both situated in a building in *Via delle Oche* but when the property was sold, all the fittings were transferred to Israel, while a new small synagogue was opened inside the Jewish school. It remains, therefore, the only one for the whole community.

THE GREAT TEMPLE

Begun in 1874 with the legacy of the defunct president of the Florentine "Università", *David Levi*, its construction took eight years and it was inaugurated in 1882 after the official visit of the King of Italy. The work of the architects *Treves, Falcini and Micheli,* the Temple (no longer synagogue, because by now only a house of prayer) of sephardic rite had at least two large scale restorations; one following the grave damage of the Second World War, the other after the terrible flood of 1966; but it remains entirely similar to the original structure. In an effort to be original and not to imitate any Christian church, the edifice is built following an exotic style,

Florence. Small temple in Via delle Oche (reproduction)

Florence. The other small temple in Via delle Oche (reproduction)

the Moorish, thus inserting a note entirely new to Tuscany and particularly to Florence.

Preceded by railings and by a fine avenue which accentuates its scenographic effect (on the right is the new Jewish school while on the boundary wall, to the left, one reads, on a plaque, the names of those deported during the last War), the building is on an elongated rectangular plan with the semi-circular apse on the short side opposite the entrances and a hemispherical dome in the centre, resting upon a high drum.

The outside, in alternating blocks of pink and white stone, is well thought out, above all in the façade. This appears in its complex tripartite form as regards both width and height; in the width, a central body, crowned by a large semi-circular arch with concave decorations, reminiscent of the Moorish, supporting the Tables of the Law, is flanked by two slightly projecting foreparts and having the form of small towers decorated with windows, and supporting two minarets on polygonal bases, with a surrounding loggia of slender columns, ending in a small dome which recalls the central one; in height, four steps precede three principal entrances in the lower part, emphasised by three Moorish arches resting on light twin columns, which open upon a shadowy narthex; on the upper level, three double windows or Moorish mullions, are separated one from another by thin pilaster strips; while on the top level, comprising the semicircular crowning arch, a wide triple mullion, surmounted by a small rose window, is flanked by two small windows perfectly in keeping. The **dome**, in a green that tones with the colours of the marble, rises on a drum, possibly too high, marked by three narrow embrasures which do not allow good internal illumination. The side walls, marked by pillars and recesses, take up, as a crowning, the wide arch of the façade and repeat the tripartite motif with variations.

The five principal entrances, three at the front and two lateral, open into a long rectangular **vestibule** with floor and walls closely decorated in mosaic and frescoes, barely lit by windows which open above the entrances themselves. Entering by the right lateral door, the floor presents huge squares with geometrical designs, the first and last two of which represent the Jewish symbol of the *"Magen David"* (Shield of David). Along the walls are placed plaques; on the left-hand wall a memorial to those fallen in the First World War; the other in Hebrew, commemorates Rabbi *Margulies* who renewed Florentine Hebraism in our century; on the right wall where there is a small marble basin for the washing of hands, an inscription recalls the visit of *Vittorio Emanuele III* on the 50th Anniversary of the Constitution of the Kingdom of Italy; in the three following medallions are recalled those who contributed to the building of the Temple with donations and the three construction architects; while the last plaque is in memory of the visit of *Umberto I and Margherita* in 1887. Through various corridors one enters the **hall of worship** true and proper. It is almost quadrangular; along three sides runs an ambulatory, while the fourth side, opposite the entrances, is occupied by the apse with the Aron. The ambulatory is limited on the three sides by the dominant motif of the entire building; three Moorish arches on twin columns, in the centre of each of which hangs an octagonal lamp. Along the lateral sections, apart from the centre of the hall, run crossways and along the wall, the benches for the faithful while windows, framed in two Corinthian columns and a Moorish arch, light them by means of polychrome panes which reproduce now and then the *Magen David*. The entire ambulatory supports the **women's gallery**, which covers the hall on three sides; it is limited by an iron balustrade, crowned by stylized *Menoròths* (7-branch candelabra), similar to the one alight on the officiant's desk. Between the arcades of the ambulatory and the gallery, on a decorative fascia, inscriptions in gold on a blue ground carry words of praise to God and devotional verses. Above the gallery wide arches on pilasters support the high drum of the dome, while in the panels, in four medallions, the gold letters are abbreviations of the words: "Who is like unto Thee, O Lord?"

The ambulatory ends in two heavy pilasters joined by an arch which thus comprises the presbytery of the apse where are the Aron and reading desk. The pulpit for sermons and addresses is backed by the left pilaster, thus distinguishing it from the Bimah.

The Apse is a vast semi-circular structure, with the bowl closely decorated, decorated along the walls, too, above and below, by the well-known motif of the Moorish triple mullion which seems almost to have a symbolical value. Between the windows the lettering on a blue ground continues in serpentine fashion. Seats for notable visitors are on the right side.

The Aron consists of a compact body; flanked by two large candelabra and preceded by four marble steps, the cabinet, on whose gilded doors are carved the Tables of the Law and the altar, is framed by six dark marble columns supporting a double Moorish arch, in the centre of which, in a medallion, is written: *"Blessed be the Glory of the Name (of God) from the place where it hath its seat"* and by a canopy panelled in mosaic on which rest the Tables of the Law. **The Bimah** is simpler, on a platform only slightly raised by three steps, closed within a balustrade of inlaid wood, it consists of a compact reading desk, right in front of the Aron. In dark wood, this has inlaid floral decorations on a gold ground; it is crowned by three candelabra, the central one of which is the Menoràh. The entire hall is frescoed, imitating the primitive mosaics, while the floor, in geometrical motifs, often repeats the Magen David.

Many treasures of art, a sign of the prosperity of the community of Florence, used to decorate the old synagogues and now decorate the present Temple: *Aronòth*, which come from small Tuscan communities now no longer existing, are kept in the small temple which stands to the right of the Great Temple. It has recently been made into a museum which following the examples of Venice and Rome, now provides a fitting resting place for the remains of community life from past centuries.

THE JEWISH MUSEUM IN FLORENCE

Florence's Jewish Museum came into being in 1981 thanks to the initiative taken by the "Friends of the Jewish Museum in Florence". It occupies a room on the first floor of the Synagogue and allows visitors to follow the historical vicissitudes of the community through photographic reproductions, and to become familiar with the characteristics of the customs and rites of Jewish groups in Florence by looking at the objects of worship on display in the show-cases.

In the **small entrance hall** some reproductions scan the prominent historical moments of past Florentine Jewish life and show its most symbolical figures.

To the left, after the reproduction of the title-page of the decree which founded the Florentine ghetto in 1570, there are some plans of the *Old Ghetto* within the context of the city, including a 16th cent. one by Bonsignori and by Billocardo, and photographs of some streets and squares in the Jewish quarter including *La Cortaccia, Piazza della Fratellanza and Piazza della Fonte.*

This iconographical collection is completed by pictures of the Italian School and Spanish School while two reproductions by Ottavio Levi recall the two oratories in Via delle Oche, outside the Ghetto, after 1888. One of these belonged to the *Mattir Assurim* Confraternity, which is also recalled by the pictures of some memorial stones and small offertory boxes.

To the right, however, it is possible to follow some moments marked by the presence in Florence of Rabbi *Margulies* who restored prestige and strength to the Jewish community in Florence at the beginning of the 20th century. His portrait, by Mario Nunes Vais, hangs next to another portrait of the famous poet *Salomone Fiorentino* (1743-1815) who was well-known among the last Italian Arcadians above all for his celebrated verses dedicated to his wife. Cultural life under the Medici is recalled by the reproduction of two 15th cent. editions of the Old Testament and by a portrait of *Elia del Medigo* (by Benozzo Gozzoli), the philosopher of the second half of the 15th century who was one of the Hebrew masters of Pico della Mirandola, while some photographs reconstruct the history of the Cemetery in Viale Ariosto up to the layouts by Marco Treves, and the building stages of the Temple in Via Farini.

After this rapid historical excursus, the liturgical reality of Florentine Jewish life is documented by bibliographical finds, documents and objects of worship.

The first case, in the centre, contains important books and documents, including some finds relative to the history of the Florentine Jewish "nation", together with 19th century material.

In a **second case, in the centre,** you can see an example of a *Sepher Torah* complete with its accessories including a *me'il* magnificently decorated on a yellow background, and a sash with floral decorations on a similarly coloured background. They are both noteworthy and belong to the middle of the 18th century. A mapàh (18th cent.) with multi-coloured floral decorations on a cream background, and a complete set of silver ornaments for the Sepher with a very beautiful *'atarah* and *rimonìm* made in Venice in 1717, also stand out. Still in the centre, a **third case**

DECRETO

ET GENERALE EDITTO

Sopra li Hebrei che al presente Habitano nel Dominio Fiorentino,

Fermato da loro Altezze. il di 26. di Settembre. 1570.

IN FIORENZA,
Nella Stamperia de' Giunti.

3

Florence, Jewish Museum. The Decree of 1570

Florence, Jewish Museum, Objects of Worship

Florence, Jewish Museum. "Paròcheth" of the Ten Commandments

displays a Sepher complete with all its ornaments: 18th cent. Florentine *rimonìm* with small superimposed towers, a decorated *'atarah* and a *me'il* dated 1720, with gold decorations on a red background. Finally, still in the centre, an *Aron* (Holy Ark) is displayed. It comes from Lippiano and dates from the end of the 18th cent. It is made of green wood, has two storeys and simple golden geometrical decorations. The objects displayed in the cases along the walls tell a slightly different story. On the right, the two-tiered first case contains objects and books relative to the Sabbath and Jewish feast-days. On the *lower level,* among the outstanding objects are an early 19th cent. embossed jug and bowl (1803), next to two examples of a *Shofàr* and a delightful small scent bottle for the day of *Kippur* (a Bolaffi donation, 19th cent.). On the upper level, on the other hand, you can see on the walls some examples of variously dated and manufactured *Chanukjòth*; a 19th cent. sabbatical lamp; a silver cover for the prayer book dating from the second half of the 18th cent. with what is probably the coat-of-arms of the family to which it belonged in the centre.

Still on the right, a **second case** contains some interesting ceremonial accessories. On the lower level many examples of *Mafthachòth* (keys) made in Florence in the 17th and 18th centuries are on display together with variously dated Florentine *yadòth* and a *mapàh* dating from the second half of the 18th century. On the upper level, on the other hand, a silver *'ataràh* dated 1769 belonging to the Italian School stands next to *rimonìms* made in the 17th and 18th centuries and to two *mapòths* dating from the second half of the 17th century.

Then on the left wall, a **first case** documents the most important moments in the family life of Tuscan Jews. On the *lower level* some interesting circumcision instruments dating from the 18th cent. (a Liscia loan) can be seen, while, on the *upper level*, two *Kethubòth*, one from Leghorn dated 1796 and one from Siena dated 1684, for the Pizarro - Cohen couple, together with two 19th century examples of prayer mantles, accompany a very beautiful 1582 bowl from the Italian School.

A **second case,** on the left displays various examples of *me'ilim*. Coming from different sources and of varying worth, they are brightly coloured and mostly belong to the 17th and 18th centuries, each one with its own sash.

The **third case** displays many interesting synagogue objects. *Rimonìm*, tablets and *mapòth*, mostly made in the 19th cent. are on display on the lower level, while on the *upper part* you can see two 17th cent. Piedmontese *rimonìm*, a 1789 *'atarah* belonging to the *Mattir Assurim* Confraternity, a *mapàh* made in Venice in about 1730 with floral decorations on a blue background.
Finally, still on the left, the most beautiful piece is displayed on the wall: a Venetian-made *paròcheth* dating from the second half of the 17th century and called *"of the Ten Commandments"*: an Aron, an unique piece of architecture, encloses the two Tables of the Law emerging from the fire, and is amply framed by small sections depicting scenes from Jewish life. It is beautifully made, a fitting crown for this iconographical collection in the Florentine Museum.

Leghorn. Temple in Via Micali. The Aron

LEGHORN

Synagogue: Via del Tempio 3

Offices of the Community: Via del Tempio 3 - Tel. 0586/896290

THE JEWS AT LEGHORN

Of the various Italian communities, Leghorn was among those which was constituted later, in the 16th cent., but also the one in which Jews enjoyed a freedom and a prestige unknown in any other Italian or Tuscan Jewish centre. The history of the Jews in Leghorn may be said to have begun, in fact, about **half-way through the 16th cent**., precisely when, because of the regulations of the Church, the Jews in Italy were passing through one of the saddest moments of their existence, because of the segregation into ghettos. **Cosimo I de' Medici,** not always bowing to ecclesiastical policy, after having regained the forts of Pisa and Leghorn, in 1541, wanted to make them into two trade centres, and issued, therefore, in 1548, a provision to attract thither as many people as possible, promising amnesties and tax exemptions, protection and religious freedom. Among others, a small group of Spanish Jews driven out in 1492 and not yet established in a fixed place, welcomed the favourable acclaim.

Leghorn. The Modern Synagogue

The port began to develop and to increase in value. **Ferdinando I de' Medici,** in 1593, renewed the invitation to merchants of every nation in a public manifesto, then called **"The Livornina",** naming explicitly first of all, the persecuted Jews and promising them remission of debts, tax exoneration, amnesties, freedom of trade and religion; not compelling them either to wear the badge or to sermons or forced baptisms, but permitting the erection of synagogues and even Tuscan citizenship, and an autonomous tribunal. Thus a larger group of Jews, above all, Spanish and Portuguese, began to flow in, enlarged two years later by a few Italian and German Jews, similarly invited. At the beginning of the 17th cent. the Leghorn community was already formed and independent, and *Meir Magino* was its consul.

With the creation of Leghorn as a free port, the most important centre for the transit of goods, many foreign "nations" took up dwelling there, but the Jewish was the richest and most important, so that at the end of the 17th cent. there were about 3,500 Jews there, destined, moreover, to double their numbers in the course of

a century. The greatest nucleus was always of "ponentini" Jews, Spanish and Portuguese, followed in order of importance, by the "levantines", while Italians and Germans were in a minority. The Iberian element and thus the Sephardic rite were meanwhile predominant; the current language was Portuguese, the literary, Castilian; important posts and administration were in Spanish hands, almost in memory of the prestige and nobility their forefathers had enjoyed in Spain. To this we must add economic prestige; they controlled the activities of the port, they were the major ships' outfitters, they introduced into the city the processing of coral, which they then exported, the soap and paper industries; they obtained tobacco contracts from the State, and possessed real estate. All this was obviously reflected in well-being and riches and in great cultural development; there were, in fact, many Jewish printing presses from which came prayer books destined later for all Italy; studies flourished with the opening of schools and of six academies *(yeshivoth)* of theological and Humanist studies; artistic expression was remarkable. Such a situation, unique in Italy, lasted till the time of Napoleon: the Medici, not as in Florence, remained ever faithful to the policy of Ferdinando and even the Lorraines who, in 1737, succeeded them, continued in this favourable attitude; furthermore, in the **second half of the 18th cent.,** the community reached its greatest splendour, to a point where many Italian Jews went there, determining, among other things, the diffusion of the Leghorn-Jewish jargon, known as *"bagito"*.

The crisis of the Jewish centre began with Napoleon. Although favourable to the ideas emanating from France, the Jewish "nation" felt the weight of the continental block imposed by the emperor, nor was it able ever to rise again. In the **first half of the 19th cent.,** the community still seemed, actually, intact in its structure, both scholastic and benevolent, but in reality they were already deprived of a total functioning; until the Leghorn Jews lost their privileges in 1859 when, with the extension of the Statute to Tuscany, their nation was made equal to all the others. The port having also ceded economic pride of place to Genoa, many emigrated to Africa and the East, leaving the community in crisis. Only in the **second half of the century** did the great Rabbi *Elia Benamozègh,* by opening a rabbinical college and conducting it wisely, lead it back for a short time to its early splendour. It was a brief interval, because only after the tragedy of the Secord World War did the community, however tried, manage to begin its great rebirth. Today it has about a thousand faithful, maintains its school and has built its new Temple.

Leghorn never had a **Ghetto**; the Jews lived in a quarter in the centre of the city, free from all regulations, often surrounded with luxury and financing at their own expense popular festivals, such as *"Mercury's Chariot"* and *"The car of the Cuccagna"*. But their well-being appeared above all in the splendid tombs of the great families and in the **great synagogue** now destroyed, judged the finest in Italy. Studying it from photographs and drawings, it seems

Leghorn. The Synagogue. Interior

to have been on a quadrangular plan, with a room surrounded on three sides by a triple order of arches, with a splendid ceiling and polychrome decoration aimed at showing off, above all, the *Aron*. Today, instead, Leghorn has a new *Great Temple*, built according to the most modern architectonic ideas, far removed from the richness of the old synagogue, but equally solemn.

THE GREAT TEMPLE

This is an extremely modern building, work of the architect *Di Castro,* inaugurated in 1962. Its plan is elliptical, divided **externally** by a continuous series of pilaster-buttresses which open almost like a corolla, giving a continuous effect of light and shade on the cement-coloured background, enlivened, however, in each section, by polygonal windows with polychrome panes.

The entrance is through a wide central portal, with geometrical reliefs, above which appear, stylized, the abbreviations of the Ten Commandments, while two *Menoròth* surmount the side entrances.

The interior, also in its squared lines, gives a sense of solemnity; the elliptical plan is more easily perceptible. *Aron* and entrance are on the same visual line and thus opposite, while the *Bimah* is in the centre of the hall, following medieval ideas. The benches for the faithful are arranged as in an amphitheatre on a semi-elliptical slope; the **women's gallery,** too, is similar, on a floor above that of the hall. The part of the ellipse not occupied by seats has the *Aron* in the centre, behind which the wall opens almost fan-like to make it stand out more. The exterior pilasters also divide the inside walls, opening at an obtuse angle, while the polygonal windows with poly-chrome panes inserted in each section thus obtained, light the hall well, enriched further in the flooring by a decorative alternation of small deep blue fields on a light ground.

As soon as one enters, one can see in the entrance hall two plaques; on the left one recalls the American associations who have contributed to the erection of the Temple; on the right one recalls its inauguration on 24 Elùl 5722, 23 September, 1962. **The Aron,** today in position, was placed there in 1970 and inserted as an antique structure in the modern complex. It comes, in fact, from the Spanish Temple of *Pesaro* and is a signed work of the beginning of the 18th cent. In wood, inlaid and heavily gilded in Baroque style, it is decorated by two small stylized columns on high plinths, support-ing a complex architrave, with decorations terminating in a structure like a reversed shell, marked by festoons. **The Bimah** is, instead, simpler; a platform raised by a small flight of steps and semi-polygo-nal balusters in polychrome marble in geometrical designs, almost recalling that of the destroyed synagogue, of the remains of which it was, in part, constructed, adding various elements of restoration.

In the underground room of the Temple has been arranged the **Lampronti Oratory;** it, too, of the Spanish rite, inserted in a rectangular room, it has *Aron* and *Bimah* on opposite sides, while entrances are on long sides, beside the latter.
Both elements come from the Spanish Temple of *Ferrara:* the **Aron** is in polychrome marble with its two doors decorated with stylized motifs and framed in twisted dark coloured columns on a high plinth, supporting the architrave in which curved lines predominate; the **Bimah** is also in polychrome marble with a balustrade fairly sim-

ilar, in complex, to that of the Upper Temple.

The rich Leghorn community donated many treasures, but among them is to be noticed, above all, *the Aron* which embellishes the **Oratory of Via Micali**; developed out of an ordinary room, the little temple has a quadrangular plan and the Bimah is substituted by a simple reading desk, but *the Aron* has a particular structure: a huge cabinet in inlaid gilded wood with floral motifs in the panels, tripartite in height and width. The central portion, the largest, contains the Scrolls of the Torah, while on top, above a projecting architrave, an imitation balustrade permits three quadrangular domes to emerge on low drums, terminanting in pinnacles. Tradition says that this was brought by Portuguese exiles who flooded into Leghorn following the *"Livornina"* and goes back perhaps to the 15th-16th cent., that is, to a moment prior to the foundation of one of the richest and most peaceful Jewish communities in Italy.

Leghorn. The Lampronti Oratory. The Bimah

Rome. Basilica of S. Pietro in Vincoli. Michelangelo, Moses

ROME

Synagogue:	Lungotevere Cenci
Permanent Exhibition:	Lungotevere Cenci
Offices of the Community :	Lungotevere Cenci - Tel 06/6840061
Kashèr Restaurants:	Tennenbaum - Via Cavour 266 Dandolo - Via Dandolo 24 "Zion" - Via Portico d'Ottavia 16

Rome. The Tiberina Island

THE JEWS IN ROME

The community in Rome is the oldest in Italy, so that for some centuries the history of Italian Jews coincided with that of Roman Jews. Different from other regions, however, the life of the Roman Jews has always been entirely conditioned by the attitude assumed in their regard by those in power; at first the fairly favourable provisions of the Empire, then the first travails with the arrival of Christianity, finally the alternating and always dramatic vicissitudes owing to the behaviour, now moderate, now intransigent and violent, of the papacy, true arbiter of Roman life up to the last century. The first contact between Rome and the Jews goes back to the Republic, when, following the mission of the Maccabees, political and economic reasons urged groups of merchants to move to the capital; but to these were added later (Ist cent. B. C.) the prisoners, then freed, brought by Pompey, who established themselves in Trastevere and constituted the first nucleus of the community. Among the oriental groups in ancient Rome, they had some privileges; Caesar allowed them public meetings, Cicero recognized their importance, even if they were small traders and artisans; Roman writers, instead, unable to understand Jewish customs were, on the other hand, always against them. The first difficulties came with the **Emperors** who, hostile in general to oriental cults, now and again expelled Jews from Rome, even if at times they confused them with the early Christians. But it was after the Destruction of the Temple (70 A. D.) that many freed prisoners

flooded into the capital, thus giving a decisive increase to the development of the community. Apart from Trastevere, they lived on the Via Appia, on the Esquilino, in the Suburra and near Porta Capena. One reads of 30,000-40,000 faithful actually, divided into at least 13 "Sinagogai" (communities) with various denominations, according to their place of origin (Tripolitania, Elea) the quarter where they lived (Suburesii, Campesii), the protector (Augustesites, Herodites): each had its own internal constitution, its own leaders and teachers, its own cemeteries in the shape of catacombs at Porta Portese, in Via Appia, Via Labicana, on Via Nomentana. They lived peacefully up to **the last years of the Empire** when, because of the continued barbarian invasions, came dramatic conditions, while, admitting that the Goths having taken Rome, showed themselves, for political reasons, favourable; that Honorius exonerated them from working on the Sabbath, giving them religious freedom; that Theodoric was always opposed to violence against them and contrary to forced conversion; that the Longobards, finally (after the difficult short interval of Byzantine rule), from 568 on, were never openly hostile to them.

But meanwhile the prestige and influence of the papacy began to be such as to condition the life itself of the Jewish; in fact, their history for about thirteen centuries is determined by the personality of each individual pope, first of all **Gregory the Great** (590-604) who, hostile to Hebraism as a religion, often sought their conversion, but by persuasion, and opposed to any violence, leaving their rights, their freedom of religion, but forbidding them to own Christian slaves. Even with the lack of information in the centuries **from the 7th-9th,** when *Charlemagne* and the overlordship of the Franks could not make their influence felt in Rome, we know, however, that often the papacy had to defend the Jews from the hostility of the clergy and from forced conversions; even though clamorous episodes were not lacking, such as that of the rich banker *Barùkh,* who was converted and whose sons Pietro and Leone took for their own the name of the *Pierleoni* family, which had given a pope to Rome; or that of *Benedict II* who allowed a persecution against the Jews, accused of having profaned sacred images (1020); on the whole, though, Jewish life, on the banks of the Tiber, ran fairly peacefully. The clergy and the papacy, later, engaged in the Crusades or the War for the Investitures, could certainly not give attention to Jews, from whom, in fact, they received economic aid; the anti-Jewish regulations, put into practice by the rest of Europe, were not enacted in Rome, nor did the community have to pay heavy tributes, up to the point where the favour of popes was shown many times and *Alexander III* (1149-81) actually had the Jew *Jechiel Anaw* as his adviser. In 1215 in the **IV Lateran Council,** under the papacy of *Innocent III,* the regulations for the segregation of Jews in a special quarter, and the wearing, as a sign, of a yellow circle by men and two blue stripes on the shawl by women were imposed, but in Rome this obligation was barely put into practice until the second half of the century. If there were also, **in the course of the 13th cent.,** difficult moments because *Honorius III* had a synagogue demolished,

Rome. Permanent Exhibition. A View of the Ghetto (from L.Rossini)

Rome. Permanent Exhibition. A Jew rolled in a Cask. (From B. Pinelli)

Gregory IX had all religious books in Europe burnt, *Charles of Anjou,* for ten years master of the city (1268-78) was hostile to them, *Boniface VIII* did not succeed in preventing the murder of Rabbi *Elia de' Pomis,* accused with all the community; if such discomforts continued during the following epoch of the "Avignon captivity" of the Papacy, when the groups who came in turn to power imposed new taxes on the Jews, urged by the regulations of Pope *John XXII,* nevertheless they did not disturb Jewish life as elsewhere and, notwithstanding favours conceded to *Cola di Rienzo* (1347) and the Plague of 1348, it returned fairly tranquil towards **the end of the 14th cent.** during the internal struggles of the Papacy.

All this favoured the development of culture and literature, and it is sufficient to remember the famous name of *Immanuel Romano,* poet in the vulgar and in Hebrew, imitator if not actually the friend of Dante; and that of Leone Romano, celebrated in the field of philosophy, or the prestige attained by many Roman Jews in the practice of medicine. At the same time, however, money-lending became more widely diffused and bankers assumed an important role, often, with their 'donations' saving the community from the danger of expulsion; even though, not finding a fertile territory for their activities in Rome, they began right then that long process of emigration which bore them to the cities of the north. The adequate safety and the respect enjoyed by the Jews living between

Rome. Permanent Exhibition. The Old Ghetto (Drawing of 1640)

Ponte S. Angelo and Ponte Quattro Capi was protracted even **into the following century**. Those popes who succeeded one another before and after the Great Schism, up **to the middle of the 16th cent.,** were at times hostile to Jews outside Rome, but in the main favourable to those inside, even if their attitude fluctuated considerably. The pontificate of *Martin V* was a happy one, defending Jewish rights, guaranteeing freedom and protection against the fiery sermons of the Franciscans and in particular of *John of Capistrano*. The danger urged Italian Jews to meet in congresses and the community of Rome had an almost directorial function. So it was that a huge sum, decided on by common accord, saved the community from the bull of *Eugenius IV* who, yielding at first, was

later on fairly strict, like *Nicholas V* who, leaving a free hand to the preachers, was opposed to the suggestion of Capistrano to transport all Jews by boat to far-off regions.

Under Sixtus IV groups of Marranos began to flood into Rome, a "Spanish" element in an entirely Italian community, which one sees notably increased: and after the expulsion from Spain under *Alexander VI* and his successors, Jews from all parts of Europe and Africa continued to flock to the capital, doubling the community numerically, but also creating internal friction between the various cults and the various jargons to the point of having to create separate synagogues, with grave internal uneasiness and continued rivalries. Only in 1524 did **Daniel da Pisa** seek, with a new administration, to bring about a solid unity. For the rest, a particularly happy period began, even if the last for Rome: Popes *Julius II, Leo X, Clement VII* were all magnanimous towards the Jews, protectors of studies, even Jewish, they, in fact, favoured the well-being of the community to a point where it managed to overcome the great danger of the Sack of Rome, caused by the *Lansquenets* in 1527 and the plague which followed, similarly with the disturbance caused by the two fanatics *David Reubenì* and *Salomon Molco* who proclaimed themselves prophets, heralds of the Messiah. It was the last positive moment before the crisis; by the 2nd half of the century, in fact, the Church, embroiled in the **Counter Reformation** and reforms, assumed a rigid and intransigent attitude. After the destruction of the Talmud, ordered by *Julius III,* anti-Jewish hatred culminated with the famous **Bull of Paul IV of 1555;** it condemned the Jews to live segregated in the Ghetto, and to have no more than one synagogue, to sell their real estate, to trade only in secondhand goods and to wear the yellow cap as a badge. The happiest and most protected community in Italy became from then on one of the most wretched; in a few months there was built, on the most dangerous banks of the Tiber, what came to be known as the *"serraglio of the Jews"*; those who could, fled, most subjected themselves to the papal hatred which soon extended to the entire Papal State. The slight relief granted by *Pius IV,* more moderate, even to instituting the famous *"Jus Gazzagà",* by which a Christian proprietor could not increase the rent of houses in the Ghetto, disappeared with *Pius V,* who not only renewed all the prohibitions, but expelled all Jews from his own State, except those of Rome and Ancona. The immigrants to the Roman Ghetto were thus numerous, and economic conditions worsened dramatically. The slight concessions of *Gregory XIII* were almost wiped out by the sermons for conversion which he instituted, while the pontificate of *Sixtus V,* under which full assurances were given, recognition of rights, enlargement of the Ghetto, commerce and immigration favoured, 64 Pawnbrokers' shops allowed: all this to find financial backing for the reform of the Church. It was, alas, but a short interval, because in 1593 *Clement VIII* rekindled the hatred and persecutions, giving rise to two centuries of oppression and squalor for the 4,000 or so Roman Jews. The misery and difficulties were due above all to heavy tributes imposed by the *Reverend Apostolic Chamber* in particular under *Urban VIII*; to the ever more humiliating regulations for the inhabitants of the Ghetto; to the debt which the Community had to contract to face up to the continued requests. More than half the faithful were living on subsidies from welfare or some fortunate family; until in 1682, *Innocent XI* abolished their last source of earning, the Credit Banks, and *Innocent XII* declared the complete bankruptcy of the community. This was the sad condition in which lived the by then over 6,000 dwellers in the Ghetto **in the course of the 18th cent.** reduced to the humblest jobs, as pedlars, secondhand dealers, in wretched shops, tailors. Nor did the moderation of *Benedict XIV* serve to better things, or the concessions of *Clement XIV* in commercial and religious fields, because at the end of the century, *Pius VI* with his *"Edict against the Jews"* (1775) caused the Ghetto to plunge into the most degrading humiliation. The minimum indulgence to the diffusion of liberal or Jacobin spirits, which was taking hold in Europe after the French Revolution, was violently repressed in Rome, and only during the Napoleonic dominion, when equal rights were granted to the Jews, could thoughts of freedom soar, which the Restoration soon frustrated. The return of the Pope meant fresh confinement, new restrictions and a state of incredible indigence.

Only under *Gregorius XVI* did some light finally appear, thanks also to the ability of *Samuel Alatri* in guiding his community. In 1848, under *Pius IX*, the gates of the Ghetto fell; the Jews entered, actually, to form part of the Constitution of the Roman Republic of '49, obtaining full equality of rights, but they did not leave the Ghetto until 1870, when the Italian troops entered Rome and by then freedom was something acquired. Rome from then on began to prosper; in 1885 the Ghetto was demolished, **Samuel Alatri** reorganized the community, and in the place that for years had witnessed their wretchedness, rose, in 1904, the great synagogue, symbol of regained splendour. In spite of the tragedy and deportations of the last War, Rome has thus recaptured its role as the first and most important Jewish community in Italy.

Rome preserves extremely old vestiges of Jewry; the most remote are the mortuary inscriptions found in the *six catacombs* so far known, and which served as underground cemeteries for the first Jews of the capital. In long passages dug out of the tufa rock, the Romans interring their dead, placed also inscriptions with symbolical designs. At *Monteverde,* on *Via Labicana, Via Appia,* near *S. Sebastiano,* on *Via Nomentana,* have been found in Greek, Latin and Hebrew, expressions of greeting such as *"Shalom"* (peace), the name and condition of the defunct, accompanied by the *Menoràh* or the *Shofàr.* Examples may be seen in the Vatican museum, or in copies at the Community's permanent Exhibition.

Little or nothing remains of the **Ghetto,** even though many Roman Jews still live in that area, between *Lungotevere Cenci, Via Catalana, Via Portico d'Ottavia.* It was, in fact, demolished in the last year of the last century to reclaim that section of the left bank of the Tiber, always exposed to the danger of floods. Instituted in 1555 by *Paul IV,* the Jews were amassed there in a few days, constrained to live wretchedly till 1848. Surrounded by walls, it had first five then seven entrances. Reproductions of the time permit one to pick out five small squares of which the most important were *Piazza Giudìa* and at least 8 streets and lanes on which faced wretched houses, forced to develop upwards or, indeed, underground, for lack of space. The names still remain of *Piazza delle Azzimelle,* because there is the oven for unleavened bread; of *Via Rua,* the main street, of *Via Reginella,* or *Via Portico d'Ottavia* (with reference to the building of Augustus in honour of his sister) near which rose the Ghetto. In such a place, tenacity was the only key to survival, and a plaque on the façade of the small *Church of S. Gregorio della Divina Pietà, quotes in Hebrew and Latin,* the lines from *Isaiah: "I have stretched out my hands all the day to a rebellious people which walketh in the dark, following their own whims".*

When they lived in the Ghetto there were many synagogues, according to the various rites; but in the last historic phase, five *"Scole"* were united in a single building, three Italian rite, **Scola**

Rome. Permanent Exhibition. A Picture of the Old Ghetto

del Tempio, Scola Nuova, Scola Siciliana; two Spanish, **Scola Catalana** and **Scola Castigliana.** All were especially rich internally with splendid furnishings and the magnificent Aronoths or the very fine ceilings as in Scola del Tempio. Destroyed to a great extent in a fire in 1893, demolished in 1910, some elements have been placed in the places of worship existing today, among which, apart from the **Oratorio Di Castro,** of Italian rite, the most important are the **Great Temple,** and that beneath, the **Spanish.**

THE GREAT TEMPLE

Built by the architects *Costa* and *Armanni* and inaugurated in 1904, the Temple in Rome rises imposingly between the present Via Catalana and Lungotevere Cenci, as a house of prayer, and lacking, as is typical of the age of emancipation, the characteristics of the old synagogue, even though, in places nearby, the administrative life of the community goes on. Of Italian rite, it manages, from an architectonic point of view to avoid possible resemblance to Christian churches, built as it is, in plan and structure, with echoes of the East and, in particular, on stylistic Assyrian-Babylonian motifs. A solid complex of centralized symmetry, with heavily squared structures projecting from the sides of a central quadrangular body, so as to create an appreciable play of masses, while in the upper part it tends to narrow, ending in a large dome.

The exterior presents solutions that vary somewhat between façade and sides. Preceded by a railing decorated by two matching capitals, having in the pediments two medallions with the Star of David, the façade, which constitutes almost a forepart, seems bipartite in height, thanks to a centralization of empty spaces; in the lower part four Assyrian-Babylonian columns, preceded by a flight of steps, give access to a vestibule in shadow, on which open the three entrances to the hall, thus following a traditional motif. On the upper level, after a crenellated molding, the same motif appears with three large windows, topped by a decorated cornice, and by a low pediment, flanked by two square capitals. Decorative elements frame the various structures, but among these stand out nearly all the symbols of Hebraism; in two squares on the sides of the windows, two stylizations of the *Lulàv*; in the middle of the pediment, amid the rays of the sun, the Tables of the Law, while in the capitals at the sides, the *Star of David,* and above, the *Menoràh.* The scheme of the pediment is repeated in the windows and in the Aron.

The lateral façade is, on the other hand, tripartite in the two senses: vertically, to one level in light ashlar with the entrances, follows the level with the three central arches, flanked by two windows, topped by a section with the same traditional motif; horizontally, the central forepart is flanked by two crenellated corner half-towers, which unite between them the façade and sides, giving the building a high volumetric value. The whole is crowned by a **dome** in four segments, in aluminium (which appears gilded) rising on a high quadrangular drum with the motif of the three windows repeated at each side and close decoration, ending in a square lantern. On the side towards the river are three *plaques,* one in memory of Jewish soldiers who fell in the 1915-18 War; another to the 2091 Roman Jews deported by the Nazis; the third to the Martyrs of the *Fosse Ardeatine* (1943). All the other plaques of the exterior have wording of biblical inspiration.

The three entrances open straight into the **hall of worship**. It is in the form of a slightly elongated quadrangle, along three sides of which runs an ambulatory, without windows, is defined by solid Assyrian columns, describing wide arcades, in the centre of which hangs a polygonal lamp. Transversely, as in all the central part of the hall, are placed seats for the faithful while the women have places in the large **women's gallery,** supported precisely by the ambulatory, which thus encloses three sides of the hall. It is defined by an iron balustrade decorated with small lamps in correspondence with the columns, while the walls have two superimposed rows of windows, separated by cornices with decorative sections in stylized floral motifs, in oriental style. Inscriptions of commemorative or biblical inspiration decorate the place: on the right, one records the visit paid to the Temple by *Vittorio Emanuele III.* In the two lateral sections two antique Aronoths have been adapted: the **Aron** on the right, modest in itself, framed by two columns and an architrave, comes from the destroyed Sicilian School

Rome. The Synagogue, Interior

Rome. The Synagogue. The Dome

and bears the date 1586; **the other,** on the left, is instead composite; with columns on a high plinth and curved architrave, it was reconstructed using pieces from various parts.

The hall receives considerable light from the vast **dome.** An architrave, resting on solid pilasters, decorated with polychrome motifs, supports a high quadrangular drum with three windows on each side, divided by sections of polychrome decoration, topped by a columned cornice with heavily decorated squares, from which rises the dome, covered with rows of varicoloured scales that diminish towards the quadrangular central lantern. This exuberant decoration is encountered also on the floor of the hall in panels arranged geometrically, but above all in the **apse** with the Aron. Defined by two massive grooved pilasters, decorated in the middle with medallions and ending in a complex structure with columns and heavily voluted capitals, the semi-hexagonal apse frames the huge aedicule of the Aron. The back wall is clearly tripartite, smooth in the lower part; the central part in squares divided by pilaster strips, each decorated with a *Menoràh* and a medallion with words of biblical inspiration, except the middle one; the upper part in decorated sections where the central square is instead substituted by an inscription. The **Aron** is framed by a heavy, much decorated aedicule; six Assyrian columns with generous volutes and gilded friezes, resting on a plinth of five steps, support an architrave with pediment which recalls in its structure the external façade, in the centre of which, with the blessing to the Name of God, is written: *"Know before Whom thou standest"*. Above, between ornamental figures and vases, are the Tables of the Law and the Crown.

The **Bimah**, instead is a wooden reading desk, inserted in the gallery surrounding the Aron; a platform raised by eight steps,

Rome. The Spanish Temple. The Aron

defined by a columned balustrade in iron and decorated with marble squares. Capitals, candlesticks and candelabra complete the decorations, while the pulpit for sermons and addresses is on the left, just below this gallery.

Thus, an imposing complex, with an exotic atmosphere, but very solemn in its majesty.

In the rooms annexed to the Temple has been inserted, among others, the **Spanish Temple.** This is reached through corridors where exhibits on the history of the Community are arranged. Elongated rectangular in form, the Aron and Bimah are on the long sides facing each other. The **Aron** is the more interesting: it comes, in fact, from the destroyed *Scola Castigliana* and is flanked by two seats with inscriptions on a black ground. The splendid gilded doors with inlaid panels are framed by two polychrome grooved Corinthian columns, on marble plinths, also polychrome, supporting an architrave with the Tables of the Law and an inscription on black ground where is blessed the Name. But the greater part of the religious objects, witness to the ancient community are collected in the

PERMANENT EXHIBITION OF THE ISRAELITIC COMMUNITY OF ROME

(The collection is subject to variations).

(The complete catalogue is distributed free at the entrance.)

At the wish of President *Pitigliani* and Rabbi *Toaff* in 1960, formed out of rooms in the Temple building, this contains, along the entrance stairs and in showcases inside, manuscripts, reproductions of old prints, valuable hangings and silverware.

Arranged according to a progressive numbering, **along the entrance stairs** there are casts of antique plaques and topographical images (1-10): among these, *two marble plaques from the Catacombs of Via Portuense,* dedicated, one to *Annis,* who was Gerusiarch of the Augustesii (1), the other one, with the four symbols of the *Shofàr,* the *Menoràh,* the *'Ethròg* and the *Lulàv,* to *Maria "who lived honourably with her husband"* (5); the inscription found in Ostia in 1962, of the 1st-3rd cent. A. D., that is, the epoch of the restoration of the first synagogue there, which reads: *"For the health of the Emperor / constructed at my own expense / the ark placed for the Holy Law / Mindis Faustos"* (6); at the foot of the stairs, with the casts of the architrave of the same Ostian synagogue, there is the base of a column and a capital of palm leaves (7-8), another testimony of the Ostian community.

In **the cases inside** are collected, first, **reproductions of manuscripts** and prints or original codices regarding Rome and its history. Among the photographic reproductions of passages from the Babylonian Talmud, apart from that in memory of *Todos di Roma,* noted for wisdom and faith (11), (13) is also interesting, describing the grandeur of 3rd cent. Rome in tones of wonder: *"with 365 markets, 3,000 baths and high walls"*.

Among the **reproductions of Hebrew texts** by Roman authors are two poetic compositions (15-16) by the famous *Immanuel Romano*, known as Manoello, who lived between 13th and 14th cent., author of sonnets in the vulgar as well as Hebrew compositions, one of which imitates the Divine Comedy of Dante.

Among the precious **original manuscripts** including the Pentateuch (17-23), that with the *Targùm* is to be admired (translation in Aramaic) (17) belonging to the Scola Catalana and going back to the 13th cent.; that with decorative elements at the beginning of each *Parashàh* (extract from Pentateuch), by *Isacco di Abramo* in Barcelona in the 14th cent. (19), and the oldest in 2 vols. (21-22), the second one containing the *Haftaròth* (extracts from the Prophets) and the 5 *Megillòths* (Scroll of the Song, Ruth, Lamentations, Ecclesiastes, Esther), written in Spain by *Josef di Samuele* at the beginning of the 13th cent. Furthermore, the fine 17th cent. *Megillàh of Esther* (25) with the blessings in panels of architectonic structure, illuminated by *Giacobbe da Castelnuovo,* and the autograph (25/A) of the 3 volumes of 30 sonnets of the famous poet *Crescenzo del Monte* (d. 1935), the most noted of those employing Jewish-Romanesque jargon in their verse.

After various documents testifying to the Nazi barbarities and going back to 1943, there are various ancient **books of prayer** or religious works in very rare editions. Among these, a formulary of the Italian rite (28) published by *Soncino* in 1486 and, with the same date and publisher, *"The book of the foundations"* (32), the philosophical-religious work of *Josef Albo.*

But the true history of the Roman Community can more easily be traced by means of the reproductions of the most important **papal bulls** or by **ancient prints** and drawings reproducing scenes of Jewish life or pictures of the old Ghetto. Thus one can see the famous bull of *Paul IV* (36) *"Cum nimis absurdum"* who, in 1555, issued the cruel anti-Jewish regulations compelling Jews, among other things, to live in the Ghetto; the edict of *Clement VIII* (39) *"Caeca et obdurata Hebraeorum perfidia"* which, in 1593, expelled Jews from all papal dominions, except Rome, Ancona, Avignon; lastly, the edict of *Gregory XIII* (41) *"Sancta Mater Ecclesia",* who, in 1584, ordained that compulsory sermons were *"to be preached to the Jews".*

Among the **prints**, on the wall, the plan of the Roman Ghetto (42) by *Zilieff* (1640); the 18th cent. print by Vasi (46) showing *Piazza Giudìa,* the most famous square in the Ghetto; a little farther along, the famous fountain in the same square (48) from the 17th cent. work of *Falda,* and *S. Maria del Pianto* (55) from a 19th cent. painting by *Ruskin.* The community had to pass through many difficult moments: compulsory sermons, as in the reproductions of the 18th cent. (45) or the watercolour by *H. Hess* (51) of the 19th cent.; now the derision of the common people, as in the reproduction of *Berneri's* poem *"Il Meo Patacca"* (49); even if it knew it had an ideal refuge in the Synagogue, a record of which is seen in a 19th cent. photograph (53).

It is, however, in the objects of worship and the **silverware,** gifts of the faithful, that one sees proofs of the devotion of the Romans. There is a splendid *silver lamp* (56), 1.65 m. tall, with three sets of branches, with embossed stem, reproducing the crest of the *Vivanti* family who donated it; three gilded cocks, a work signed by *Vanneschi,* going back to the late 18th cent. Among the **Yadoths** (indexes for the Sepher) (57-69); in silver-gilt (65) in the form of *Lulàv* is the very lovely, 18th cent. work by the same *Vanneschi,* with the crest of the donor, *Uzielli,* two lions rampant; and that, still 18th cent. in silver-gilt (67), with a fine diamond on the index, and on the first knot the crests of the lion, the star and the moon. Very rich indeed is the collection of ornaments for the Sepher: among the **Rimonìm** (terminals) (70-89) the one given to the *Scola Catalana* halfway through the 17th cent. is charming (71), a pomegranate with a crest with orb and crown supported by lions rampant; and the 19th cent. ones of *Scola del Tempio* (76) in silver-gilt, having in panels, the lamp of the Sabbath and the blessing hands of the officiant, ending in flowers; but the variety is truly great, some have the form of lanterns, with towers, lions and symbols (74, 81, 82, 84, 86, 87) decorated with flowers and columns; or the form of a tower (77, 89) with candelabra and niches; or more elaborate (78, 79, 85, 88) often work of noted goldsmiths and artists adapted to Jewish tradition. Among the **'Ataròth** (crowns) (90-104) and *semi-crowns* (105-114) there is equal variety: most interesting are the most antique, all of the 17th cent.: that in silver-gilt with lions and candelabra, inscriptions and polychrome stones (93), gift of the *Di Segni* family; the small one, chiselled, with stones and inscriptions, gift of the *Del Monte* family (94); that given by the *Ascarelli* family (99), pierced, with floral motifs, towers and two lions; but all the others, bearing the common symbols and the known ornaments, constitute a worthwhile patrimony. The same elements are found in the semi-crowns, among which, however (110), is an eccentric 18th cent. one given to the *Scola del Tempio* and bearing in a crest a camel and a star, *Stella Cammeo* being, in fact, the donor.

For this reason certain splendid **jugs and basins** used for the washing of hands by the priests before the benediction, stand out particularly (115-119); among them (118), in the style of a lion, who, raised on his hind legs, bears the shield with the crest of the *Tedeschi* family, a *Menoràh*, a column and a lion; it is accompanied by an embossed wash-hand-basin in hexagonal form, with shell decorations, and a lion and a Menoràh in the middle, of German workmanship of 17th-18th cent.; one may add various **goblets and chalices** (120-126) in finely worked silver, but above all a striking **Chanukjàh** (9-branch candelabrum) (127), wall type, 18th cent., embossed silver, decorated with floral and fruit motifs, and bearing, in the centre, above the eight lights, an antique-style *Menoràh;* and various **silver covers** for prayer books (130-137), all 18th cent., all decorated with the crests of the donors and floral motifs, among which (130) is outstanding from the *Scola del Tempio,* embossed, with vases of flowers, emblems and crowns, bearing, in the five panels at the back, four crests and the *Menoràh.*

Less noticeable, but equally beautiful, certain **Mafthachòth** (keys for the Ark) (138-141), in silver or bronze with the *Magen David;* some **cradle medals** and **plaques** (141-151), while certain **parochiòth** (curtains for the Aron) (152-155) are interesting, among them a Florentine one belonging to the *Scola Catalana* (153) of the 16th cent. in red brocade with designs in gold, geometrical panels, and above, the Tables of the Law, on a ground of blue-gold; the Venetian one of the same century (154) belonging to *Scola Nuova,* with frame and embroidery on three columns in floral motifs. Nearby are certain **coverings for the tribune** in brocade or embroidery (156-159), while among the various **me'ilìm** (vestments for the Sepher) (160-167) stand out the Venetian ones of the 17th cent. (162-163) in brocade or velvet, with embroidery, emblems and crests; and nearby a **Mapàh** (cover for the Sepher) (168), Florentine 16th cent. in red satin with embroidery and in the centre a crest with a tree.

The exhibition is completed with some examples of **Chairs for milòth** (circumcisions), called *"Chairs of the Prophet Elijah"* (174,175,176) and various reproductions and paintings of small value.

However, one cannot have a complete picture of what the oldest Italian community was like unless one considers also the Jewish nucleus of *Ostia Antica,* the port of Rome which recently has restored to knowledge possibly the oldest known synagogue. It is of such great importance that it is given a special report.

Rome. Ancient Synagogue in Trastevere.

Rome. The Temple in Via Balbo

JEWS AT OSTIA ANTICA

Even before the destruction of the Temple of Jerusalem (70 A.D.) considerable groups of Jews had become established in the most important commercial centres of the Mediterranean. Above all, the greatest ports saw the building up of Jewish nuclei which in part assimilated with the pagan population, in part remained distinct from it as regards way of life and religion. Thus, after having formed prosperous communities in *Elephantina, Alexandria,* Antioch and the ports of North Africa, they came also to the principal sea towns of North and South Italy, and just as a community certainly flourished in *Aquileia* (in the North Adriatic) similarly a Jewish nucleus formed in the port of Rome, **Ostia.**

Founded, according to legend, by the King *Ancus Marcius,* where Aeneas landed, but according to archaeological reports, in the 4th century B. C. it was first a port of great military importance, then an even greater commercial port. Enlarged at the end of the Republic, in imperial days *Claudius* began the works for the artificial port which Nero then inaugurated and Trajan (2nd cent. A. D.) enlarged again. Thus it became Rome's fluvial port, with all the characteristics of sea towns; a heterogeneous and cosmopolitan population, very lively, flourishing development of houses and temples, interweaving of various religious cults. In the period of its greatest splendour (1st-3rd cent. A. D.) there were many eastern cults in Ostia (Serapis, Mithras, etc.) and among these, certainly the Jewish religion as well.

Until a few years ago, the presence of Jews in Ostia was uncertain. As proof, there were certain names found in epigraphs, a lantern of the type used by Jews, certain inscriptions found in the nearby *Port,* the city built by *Claudius,* but not from definite sources, then more important, a mutilated epigraph of the 2nd cent. found at *Castel Porziano*, ten kilometres from the port, in which it is believed that the words missing in the first line can be integrated with the expression ."*The University of the Jews who are established in the Colony of Ostia*". But it was all too little. Now, following the discovery of the fine synagogue, the presence of a prosperous Jewish community at Ostia is certain. When it was formed cannot be said with certainty; one may, instead, suppose what were its internal constitutions and what the social position of its members, taking for example the nearby Rome, with whom relations were certainly very close.

In spite of the hostility shown towards them by Roman writers and intellectuals, the Jews were able to enjoy, at Ostia, too, a certain freedom. They were socially of the middle class, nearer, therefore, to the common people than to the upper classes; they followed modest trades, were blacksmiths, tailors, butchers, actors, but above all they were small tradesmen who, being free, enjoyed civil rights, even without being able to reach the upper grades. Given the particular development of the port, however, their condition was

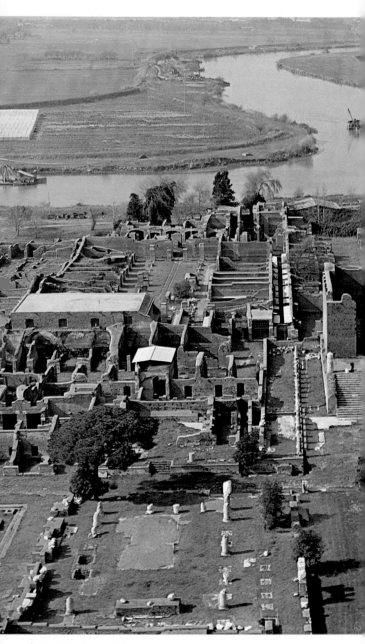

Ostia Antica. General View

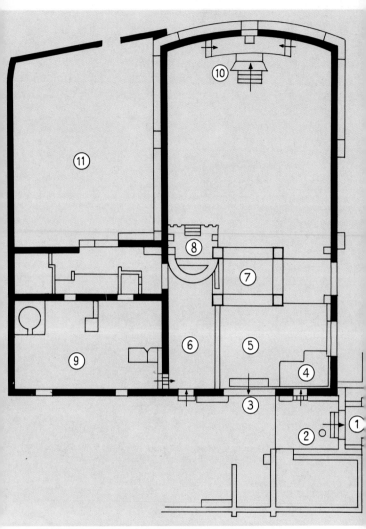

PLAN OF THE OSTIA ANTICA SYNAGOGUE

1 Entrance from Via Severiana
2 Section showing the well
3 Middle entrance
4 The Mikvah
5 Front central section
6 Area reserved for women
7 The four central columns
8 The Aron
9 Area with the oven
10 The podium
11 The area with the benches

Ostia Antica. The Synagogue. The "small" well

Ostia Antica. The Synagogue. Inscription of Mindis Faustos (cast)

without doubt better than that of the Roman community, so much so as to let them build, maintain and readapt for about three centuries a fine synagogue. The community must have been fairly numerous, possibly five hundred of them, organised as in the community of Rome, but making up an autonomous and independent organism. With its own spiritual centre in the synagogue, the community was administered by a *"gerousia"* and by a council of *"presbyteroi"*, a kind of president and council of the elders; executive powers were in the hands of the *"archons"* while in the religious field the greatest authority was represented by the *"archisynagogus"* who had to look after the functioning of the houses of prayer and the administration of sacred goods. Basically this was the rabbi of today, who was also teacher and judge.Thus, a compact structure which explains the presence of a vast articulated edifice which, even today, offers the only example of synagogal remains of certain identification in Italy, going back to such a remote epoch.

Ostia Antica. Synagogue. View showing entrances

THE SYNAGOGUE OF OSTIA ANTICA

The synagogue of Ostia Antica is, among those known, the oldest in Europe and possibly in the world. It was discovered in 1961-62 following two happy excavation campaigns carried out in the area of the road curve where *Via Calza* runs into *Via della Scafa,* and its identification remained uncertain till the discovery of two architraves with some of the best known Jewish symbols. The building, apart from the hall of prayer true and proper, is made up of several rooms adapted for various uses demanded by Jewish tradition; study hall, oven for azyme bread, ritual bath, possibly a small rabbinical tribune, and this goes back to the old meaning of synagogue, understood as centre of the entire life of a community. The wall structure, of various techniques, shows that the building visible today (4th cent.) rose on another edifice of a preceding epoch, but having a similar plan, going back to the 1st cent. A.D.

and the fortunate discovery of an inscription, referring to this earlier building, but readapted to the floor plan of the second, also confirms that the earlier one, too, was a synagogue. We have, thus, an exceptional synagogal complex; a small synagogue built in *"opus reticulatum"* going back to the 1st cent. A. D. and above it, with much readaption, using the walling technique of *"opus vittatum"* (3rd-4th cent. A. D.) a second synagogue, around which was built also the vast complex of rooms adapted to particular uses. Which covers in all, an area of about 1,000 square metres.

But let us visit the various points, in order.

Ostia Antica. Synagogue. Hall of Worship. Side-view

The location: The synagogue rose at the end of the decuman of the city of Ostia, near the ancient river bank. It is parallel to the edge of the old port and to *Via Severiana*, the important coastal artery. The hall thus follows the custom, common above all during the Dispersion, of rising near the sea or a watercourse, so that the water for the prescribed ablutions might arrive by "natural" means into the ritual bath (and the little well to be seen on the left of the entrance, above a cistern, demonstrates this), and in the second place, outside the city, so as not to injure the susceptibilities of the Romans who, while not obstructing such buildings, wanted them outside the "pomerium".

The entrance: This is in *Via Severiana.* Through an entry marked by two steps, one finds oneself in an elongated rectangular vestibule, on the right side of which open the three entrances to the hall of worship and the two to the place where the oven is located; while on the left side there are small rooms difficult to identify. Possibly, for the first one only of these, one might suggest the hypothesis that it was a tank or bath. But the most interesting part of this narthex is really the short side of the entrance. The two steps are preceded by two quadrangular sub-bases, faced in marble, on which rested columns to ornament the door, which, united, possibly formed a porch. Beyond the steps one finds a paved area, beneath which opens a cistern visible through a marble well. From the upper edge down to the ground, this presents a not very regular curved grooving, which has a certain effect, reproducing a decorative motif widely diffused in ancient Rome.

The façade: The right side of the narthex is occupied by the façade of the synagogue: the wall structure shows that it goes back to the 3rd-4th cent. A. D. Like the synagogues of Galilee, it has three entrances; the central one, probably wide and monumental, gives access to the hall of worship true and proper, the side ones, instead, lead to two sections; that on the right, identifiable as the *"Mikvah"* or ritual bath, that on the left, to a raised hall, possibly destined for the women. It must have been decorated because, as in the ancient synagogues, it is really the side turned towards Jerusalem, in this case to South South-east. This signified that the builder of the synagogue was compelled to place the Aron in a rather strange position, in the central part of the hall, on the left in a contrary sense to the way of entry.

The two buildings: Before proceeding with the visit to the hall of worship, let us consider the presence of two synagogues, going back to different periods. The hall, in fact, an elongated rectangle in form, with the end wall slightly curved, as it appears now, came from enlarging and modifying, as we know, the structures of a previous building. The different wall structures allow us to fix a date. The first building is in *"opus reticulatum"*, that is, small blocks shaped like truncated pyramids, arranged in lines sloping at an angle of 45°, and thus goes back to the 1st cent. A. D. when this technique was used in Ostia. The second is in *"opus vittatum"*, that is, formed of small tufaceous bricks arranged in regular horizontal rows, and goes back to the epoch of diffusion of this technique, 3rd-4th cent. A. D. The first building was smaller and reduced to the dimensions of the present hall of worship; the second, much larger, with vestibule and annexed rooms. It is the only remaining example in the dispersion of two superimposed synagogal buildings.

The 1st cent building: The hall of worship corresponding to the present one was preceded by an atrium-vestibule, of which one can still see the rubblework flooring and the line of the benches

Ostia Antica. Synagogue. The Aron

which ran along the walls; each internal division, however, belonged to a later epoch. It had the same characteristics as those visible, with four central columns, standing closer, however, perhaps defining a monumental entrance and with benches for the faithful along the walls.The Aron, since there is no trace of a structure like that of the 4th cent. was certainly mobile, which is confirmed by an inscription on a marble slab, reutilised in the flooring of the second synagogue, saying, in Latin for the first line and ' Greek for the rest:

For the health of the Emperor
I constructed and made at my own expense
The Ark placed for the Holy Law
Mindis Faustos.

In this, to indicate the Sacred Ark, is used the Greek term *"kibo-*

tos", which means *"Wooden cabinet"*, presumably transportable. The inscription, going back to the 2nd cent. A.D., apart from telling us that the edifice was a synagogue, names a notable person of the time, the only name remaining to us of the community of Ostia.

The Synagogue of the 4th cent.: The Hall: Similar in its external structure to the previous edifice, even though this appears sometimes to be reinforced with pilasters and sometimes doubled with brick facing, it differs by reason of the internal solution. The floor is on different levels which appears to divide it into two parts at the height of the four central columns: the floor at the lower level is in mosaic, the upper in marble. The hall is thus made up of a front part in three sections, with an architectonic dividing partition, formed of four columns and by the aedicule of the Torah, and of a back part, spacious and without internal divisions.

But let us examine the single sections.

The front part, between the entrance and the columns, seems divided into three sections by two stone balustrades going back to the 2nd-3rd cent. when the primitive synagogue was restored. **The section on the left** is almost a part by itself, closed between the left hand entrance to the synagogue, the wall next to the oven and the apse of the Aron. Its floor, in white mosaic with a black ornamental strip running round, is raised. Since the women, in the old synagogues, were separated from the men, finding a place on a *"platform"* that looked towards the inside of the temple or in a gallery, it is probable that this "corridor" was properly designed for the faithful who could attend the ceremonies from outside.

The right-hand section, which one reaches going down two steps, is also separated from the rest of the hall, by a low balustrade-wall; its walls are in *"opus reticulatum"*, except for the jambs and the corner which are in *"opus vittatum"*. It is faced by marble veneer and marked by a projecting plinth; the floor, well preserved, is hollowed in one part possibly to form a basin, for the rest it is in mosaic of simple workmanship, with the motif of the rose widely diffused in Jewish ambients. It is easy to recognise in the hollowed section the *Mikvah* or ritual bath of the synagogue, into which water flowed from the nearby well, or was drawn from the water reserves recognizable in the annexed ambients.

Finally, **the central section** is the least interesting, even if the only one allowing access to the hall through the columns. However, in its mosaic flooring now destroyed, remains, near the entrance, the only mosaic representation of the synagogue: a panel with a chalice and a figure not clearly recognizable but possibly identifiable as a loaf, chalice and bread being connected in the ceremony of *"Kiddush"*, (consecration).

The four columns which rise on almost the same point as that in the preceding building, about 4.70 m high, are of grey marble with slightly tapering shafts and Corinthian capitals in white marble, well made and with interesting effects of light and shade. Their particular position does not allow of a safe identification of their function: possibly they were to mark the monumental entrance to the hall of prayer, because it is fairly difficult to accept the hypothesis that, together with two other columns found out of place, they made a division of the hall itself into three naves, something which moreover constitutes a strange solution which finds no echo in other synagogues of the time.

To the left of the columns immediately on entering the hall is the **aedicule of the Aron**, the strangest structure in the building: a high platform in *"opus sectile"*, preceded by four steps, and an apse oriented to southeast, in *"opus vittatum"* with two end pillars, closed by a little wall raised against the ground; the whole is preceded by two slightly tapered columns with composite capitals. Between the pillars of the apse and the columns are two corbelled architraves which have Jewish symbols sculptured on them. They are certainly the most interesting elements in the synagogue. Obtained from earlier pieces, with the external sides decorated by a flat cornice, on the inside the two architraves present two rectangular hollows made to support a wood partition which possibly supported a *"paròcheth"* (curtain for the Aron) with in the front part the symbolic figures: the *"Menoràh"* (7 branch candelabrum) symbol of Hebraism itself; the *"Shofàr"* (ram's horn) whose sound called for obedience and faith in God; the *"Lulàv"* (palm branch) and the *"'Ethròg"* (citron fruit), together linked to the Feast of Booths (*Sukòth*). They are carved somewhat roughly, in low relief, descriptively, with everything reduced to essentials, but having been at one time embellished with gilding. Although original, the Aron responds to the rule of orientation towards Jerusalem, having obviously been inserted in a pre-existing building in the best way possible.

Beyond the four columns comes finally **the hall** real and proper. It presents a structure of walling with facing, and flooring in polychrome tiles arranged geometrically; on the curved end wall is a **podium** constructed in successive phases with access at front and side. It was possibly the Bimah of the synagogue, or more probably the place where the notable people sat. The internal space, which the wall partly raised again brings back to life, gives a sense of grandeur and solemn immobility without movement of light, almost as if to indicate the Divine presence. This, too, might suggest that the two columns found out of place used to frame the podium, but not that they divided this still and static place into naves.

The annexed rooms: As in other ancient synagogues, many rooms, adapted to various uses, but nevertheless, linked with religion, surround the hall. Among these, the most interesting are: the room which rises in continuation of the façade of the synagogue, on the left; it is rectangular, fairly large, going back to the primitive building. It has, however, been adapted, in succeeding centuries, closing one of its two entrances, constructing a bench with a marble slab and in the opposite corner, an oven with a pudding stone vault. Even the primitive flooring, in black and white mosaic, has been covered with a rough flooring in lime and beaten earth. It was evidently **the oven** in which was prepared, for the community, and possibly for other Jewish groups nearby, the azyme bread for Easter *(Pésach)*.

At the side of this, along its longest side, opens a corridor which joins the synagogue to a vast room to which access is gained by an opening behind the Aron: with benches along one side, it was possibly, not only a passage but a waiting place. From it one enters a huge room flanking the hall of worship built in the 3rd-4th cent.; along the walls run benches and the floor presents small traces of mosaic; it was a **hall of study or assembly**, where the faithful met, under the guidance of a teacher, to study the Torah.

Following this room, behind the end wall are many other rooms; among them a small rectangular room with wide entrance and benches along the walls, gives access to a quadrangular area with a seat hollowed out at the centre of each of the free walls. If this could be identified as a **"Beth Din" (rabbinical tribune),** Ostia would truly offer the most complete example of a synagogue, understood as the centre of a Jewish community.

Aron	Holy Ark to hold the Scrolls of the Torah.
Ashkenazic	German Jew or German rite
'ataràh	Crown, ornament for the Scroll of the Torah
Beth Din	Law Court, tribunal
Beth ha Kenéseth	Meeting House, Synagogue
(Beth) Midràsh	House for Bible Comment; rabbinical seminary
Bimah	Podium, officiant's tribune
Chanukàh	Inauguration. Festival of 25 Kislev (December) which recalls the heroism of the Maccabees, celebrated by lighting the 9-branch lamp
Chanukjàh	9-branch Candelabrum lit during the festival of Chanukàh
Chuppàh	Canopy for the bridal pair
Elùl	Jewish month - August-September
'Ethròg	Citron fruit, traditional in the Feast of Booths (Sukòth)
Haftaròth	Extracts from the Prophets which are read after the public reading of the Sepher
Hazàn	Cantor, officiant in the Synagogu
Kéther	Crown, sign of majesty
Kethubòth	Marriage contracts
Kiddush	Consecration; this is done with a glass of wine, reciting the prescribed benedictions
Lulàv	Palm branch, traditional in the Feast of the Booths (Sukòth) with 'Ethròg
Mafthachòth	Keys to open the Holy Ark
Magen David	Shield of David, the 6-pointed star, typical Jewish symbol
Mapàh	Cloth, rectangle of material used to cover the Sepher
Mazàh	Unleavened bread which is eaten during the 8 days of Pésach (Easter)
Megillah	Scroll, traditionally the Book of Esther. By "Chamèsh Megilòth" - Five Rolls- is understood: The Song, Ruth, Lamentations, Ecclesiastes, Esther.
Me'il	Vestment, mantle for the Scrolls of the Sepher
Menoràh	7-branch candelabrum, the most common symbol of Hebraism
Mikvah	Bath, tub where are carried out ritual ablutions for purification
Milàh	Circumcision; generally 8 days from birth

Ner Tamid	Perpetual light, which remains lit in front of every Aron
Parashàh	Portion of the Pentateuch, according to the traditional division, read in the Synagogue
Parnàs	Superintendent of the Synagogue
Paròcheth	Curtain placed in front of the Aron
Pésach	The Jewish Easter, celebrated on 15th Nisàn (April), in memory of the deliverance from Egypt
Purìm	Feast of Lots; celebrated 14th Adàr (Feb.-March) in memory of the salvation, obtained by Esther against the cruelty of the Persian, Haman
Rimòn	Pinnacle, terminal ornament for the Sepher
Rosh ha Shanàh	New Year; 1st Tishrì (Sept.-Oct.)
Sephardic	Spanish, Spanish rite
Sepher	Book, for antonomasia, the Scrolls of the Torah
Shadài	Omnipotent. This is written on certain medallions for the cradles of the new-born.
Shalòm	Peace. The most common Jewish greeting
Shofàr	Ram's horn, whose sound calls folks to God
Simchat Torah	Joy of the Torah, when ends and begins again the reading of the Torah
Sukòth	Feast of Booths which begins 15th Thishrì (Sept.-Oct.), connected with agriculture and the sojourn of the Jews in the desert
Talmud	Complex of traditions and rabbinical discussionsabout the Torah
Talmud Torah	Jewish school of religious foundation
Targùm	Translation of the Pentateuch into Aramaic
Tas	Ornamental plaque for the Sepher
Thevàh	Commonly used as synonym of Bimah
Thìq	Case for the Scrolls of the Torah
Torah	The Law, the complex of precepts which regulate Jewish life (lit. Teaching)
Yad	Hand, index for the reading of the Sepher
Yeshivàh	Academy, place of senior religious studies

VISITING TIMES OF SYNAGOGUES AND MUSEUMS

VENICE:
From June to September 10 a.m. - 7 p.m.
From October to May 10 a.m. - 4.30 p.m.
Closed on Saturdays and Jewish Holidays; Fridays one hour before closing time.

Guided Visits:
a.m. 10.30 - 11.30 - 12.30, p.m. 1.30 (only English) - 2.30 (p.m. 3.30 - 4.30 - 5.30)
The box office closes one hour before closing time.
Ticket: Museum plus Synagogues plus guide L. 12.000, L. 9.000 reduction
Groups are kindly requested to book in advance.
Apply to the Museum of Jewish Art.
Ghetto Nuovo Cannaregio 2902/B- Tel. 715359 Fax 723007

FLORENCE:
Synagogue: from April to September from Sunday to Thursday 10 a.m.- 1 p.m., 2-5 p.m.; Friday 10 a.m. - 1 p.m.; from October to March from Monday to Thursday 10 a.m. - 1 p.m., 2-4 p.m.; Friday 10 a.m. - 1 p.m.; Saturday closed; Sunday 10 a.m. - 1 p.m.

Closed on Jewish holidays, Jan. 1, May 1.

Ticket: L. 6.000; L. 4.000 reduction for students and groups, maximum 15 persons

Apply to the Offices: Sezione didattica Museo Ebraico, Via Farini, 4 - Tel. (055) 2346654

LEGHORN:
Closed: on Friday afternoon and on Saturday
Ticket: L. 5.000.
Apply to the Offices of the Community
Piazza Elia, 1 (ask for Benamozegh)
Tel. (0586) 896290
Fax. (0586) 896290

ROME:
From October to May 9 a.m. - 2 p.m.; 3-5 p.m.; from June to September 9.30 a.m. - 2 p.m.; 4-6 p.m.;
Sunday 9-12.30 a.m.

Closed Jewish holidays.

Ticket: L. 5.000, L. 3.000 reduction.
Lungotevere Cenci - Tel. (06) 6875051.

OSTIA:
10a.m. -5p.m. Open all day except Monday.

CONTENTS

Storti Edizioni srl
Via Brianza 9/C - 30030 Oriago di Mira - (VE) - (Italy)
Tel. 041.5659057 - 041.5659058
Fax 041.5631157
www.stortiedizioni.it
e-mail: edstort@tin.it